Educational Research

Also available from Bloomsbury

Teacher Agency: An Ecological Approach
Reinventing the Curriculum: New Trends in Curriculum Policy and Practice
Jacques Rancière: Education, Truth, Emancipation
Thinking in Education Research: Applying Philosophy and Theory
Philosophy of Educational Research

Educational Research

An Unorthodox Introduction

Gert Biesta

BLOOMSBURY ACADEMIC
LONDON • NEW YORK • OXFORD • NEW DELHI • SYDNEY

BLOOMSBURY ACADEMIC
Bloomsbury Publishing Plc
50 Bedford Square, London, WC1B 3DP, UK
1385 Broadway, New York, NY 10018, USA

BLOOMSBURY, BLOOMSBURY ACADEMIC and the Diana logo are trademarks
of Bloomsbury Publishing Plc

First published in Great Britain 2020

Cover design: Adriana Brioso
Cover image © Nationaal Archief/Collectie Spaarnestad/Wiel van der Randen

A catalogue record for this book is available from the British Library.

ISBN: HB: 978-1-3500-9798-8
PB: 978-1-3500-9797-1
ePDF: 978-1-3500-9800-8
eBook: 978-1-3500-9799-5

Typeset by Deanta Global Publishing Services, Chennai, India
Printed and bound in India

Contents

Acknowledgements

In writing this book I have made use of material that was earlier published as follows: Biesta, G. J. J. (2015). No paradigms, no fashions and no confessions: Why researchers need to be pragmatic (pp. 133–49). In A. B. Reinertsen & A.M. Otterstad (Eds), *Metodefestival og Øyeblikksrealisme*. Bergen: Fagbokforlaget; Biesta, G. J. J. (2016). Improving education through research? From effectiveness, causality and technology, to purpose, complexity and culture. *Policy Futures in Education* 14(2), 194-210; Biesta, G. J. J. (2010). Why 'what works' still won't work. From evidence-based education to value-based education. *Studies in Philosophy and Education* 29(5), 491–503; Biesta, G. J. J. (2013). Knowledge, judgement and the curriculum: On the past, present and future of the idea of 'the practical'. *Journal of Curriculum Studies* 45(5), 684–96; Biesta, G. J. J. (2011). Disciplines and theory in the academic study of education: A Comparative Analysis of the Anglo-American and Continental Construction of the Field. *Pedagogy, Culture and Society* 19(2), 175–92; Biesta, G. J. J. (2017). Education, measurement and the professions: Reclaiming a space for democratic professionality in education. *Educational Philosophy and Theory* 49(4), 315–30; Biesta, G. J. J. (2014). Pragmatising the curriculum. Bringing knowledge back in, but via pragmatism. *The Curriculum Journal* 25(1), 29-49; Biesta, G. J. J. (2012). Knowledge/Democracy. Notes on the political economy of academic publishing. *International Journal of Leadership in Education* 15(4), 407–20. I am grateful to the original publishers for the possibility to make use of this material.

About the Author

After a not entirely successful time in secondary school and higher education, Gert Biesta (www.gertbiesta.com) worked in a hospital where he became involved in the education of radiographers, mainly teaching (applied) physics. He returned to higher education as a mature student and obtained a degree in the theory and history of education and a degree in the philosophy of the social sciences. After this, he worked on a PhD on the work of John Dewey, which he successfully defended in 1992. He worked at several universities in the Netherlands before moving to England in 1999 and to Scotland in 2007, with positions in Scotland, Luxembourg and England. In 2019 he was appointed (part-time) Professor of Public Education at Maynooth University, Ireland, and (part-time) Professorial Fellow in Educational Theory and Pedagogy at the Moray House School of Education of the University of Edinburgh. In addition, he holds the (part-time) NIVOZ Chair for Education at the University of Humanistic Studies, the Netherlands, and is visiting professor at the University of Agder, Norway. He has held visiting professorships in Sweden, Norway and Belgium, and has been editor-in-chief of the journal *Studies in Philosophy and Education*. Currently he is co-editor of the *British Educational Research Journal* and associate editor of *Educational Theory*. Gert Biesta has published extensively on the theory of education and the theory and philosophy of educational research, with a particular interest in questions of democracy and democratization. His work has so far been published in twenty different languages.

Foreword

In this book I raise questions about educational research that are often forgotten in the ways in which novice researchers are introduced to the field. While I do not seek to provide an alternative to such 'orthodox' introductions, I do hope that this book may help to broaden the perspective of beginning educational researchers on the field they are entering, so that they can conduct their research in a more thoughtful way, which, as I argue in this book, can also mean that they refrain from conducting research in those situations where something else is needed. The ideas presented in the book stem from my own research experience and the many conversations I have had with students and fellow educational researchers, also in the contexts of courses in research methods, approaches and designs. I am particularly grateful to the students I have taught over the years, as they have helped me greatly in refining and sharpening up the arguments I seek to present in this book. I would like to thank Mark Richardson at Bloomsbury for his confidence in this project and also for his patience. And I would like to thank the anonymous reviewers of the proposal and the full manuscript for their encouragement and helpful feedback.

Edinburgh, March 2019.

Prologue: The Orthodoxies of Educational Research

Many students in education who embark on a research project will, at some stage in their trajectory, encounter views about what research is about, what good research is and what the right way of doing research is. One is told, for example, that there are research paradigms and that it is important to choose a paradigm and locate one's research within it. Or that there is a fundamental difference between quantitative and qualitative approaches and that one either needs to make a choice for one of them or, as has become popular in recent times, adopt a mixed approach. Or that there is a need to articulate the epistemological and ontological assumptions that inform one's research. Or that one needs to select a theoretical framework for the research, often stemming from disciplines such as psychology, sociology or philosophy. And that educational research should not only be good research in itself but should ultimately also contribute to the improvement of educational practice.

Over the years many books have been published that aim to help students in designing and doing their research, and there is still an increasing number of websites and internet-based resources that seek to do the same. Many of these books and resources focus on the practicalities of research, such as how to formulate good research questions; how to collect data and how to analyse them; how to draw valid conclusions; how to deal with research ethics and how to get one's research published. In addition, there are books and resources – fewer in number – which deal with underlying issues and assumptions, particularly philosophical questions about the nature of knowledge (epistemology) and social reality (ontology) and the norms and values that should guide research (ethics).

What is remarkable about these materials is the strong convergence towards a small number of themes, issues and message which, together, construct a kind of 'common sense' of what it means to do research in education. They not only are part of the everyday vocabulary about research – the way people talk about the design and conduct of their research – but also frame a set of more or less explicit expectations for everyone who wishes to engage in educational research. Meeting these expectations can even be seen as a rite of passage for novice researchers, something they have to go through in order to become recognized members of the educational research community. In this regard they are literally the orthodoxies of educational research in that they depict the right (*orthos*) understanding (*doxa*) of what educational research is about, what it is for and what would count as good research.

While the many books, resources and courses in research methods are obviously trying to be helpful, students nonetheless struggle. The requirement to articulate one's epistemological and ontological assumptions, for example, often results in rather bland and often misguided claims and statements about issues that philosophers have been arguing over for centuries, and continue to be in discussion about. The requirement to locate one's research in a particular research paradigm often results in confessional statements – 'I am a qualitative researcher', 'I am a social realist', 'I am a post-structural feminist' – rather than that there are informed discussions about what it would mean to locate one's research in the first place and about how much choice there actually is. Similarly, theoretical frameworks are often chosen because they are 'around' or, 'even worse', because they are the latest fashion, rather than that researchers begin with the question of how much and what kind of theory one actually needs to achieve one's research ambitions. And while, for a long time, research was either quantitative or qualitative, with heated debates between the two camps, now it seems as if almost all research has to make use of mixed methods, often without really engaging with the question what such mixing actually entails. Also, where almost all research in education seeks to contribute to the improvement of practice – and rightly so, in my view – there is often a lack of reflection of what it means to improve educational practice and how research might help rather than hinder.

There is, of course, no point in blaming students for this state of affairs, as in most cases they have just been exposed to these orthodoxies and also know that their research will be judged in terms of whether they have met the expectations contained in these orthodoxies sufficiently well. If anyone – or anything – is to blame, we probably need to look in the direction of the materials and courses that are being produced to introduce students to the theory and practice of research. While I do not want to discredit such materials – they are well intended, and it is of course important to find out what the right way of doing research is – there are, however, questions that are less often asked or sometimes just remain absent in much of the literature on the *how*, the *what* and the *what for* of educational research. The essays brought together in this book are precisely meant to focus on the marginal and sometimes forgotten dimensions of what educational research is, what it might be for, what it can achieve and where there are limits that researchers should be mindful of as well.

This book does not provide an alternative introduction to educational research, and even less so an introduction to alternative ways of doing educational research. It is rather meant to raise questions and explore issues that are often absent in more orthodox introductions to the field. It should therefore be read *alongside* such introductions and not in place of them. This book is not intended to discredit those introductions, but rather seeks to provide a perspective on them, so that a more thoughtful and perhaps more critical engagement with the orthodoxies of educational research may become possible. The book is first of all meant for students, that is, for those who are entering the field of educational research. But beyond this, the book is also intended to raise issues for the wider educational research community about what research is, how we can best articulate our ambitions with research and how we can keep a focus on the specific nature of educational research so that research can indeed live up to its expectation at the improvement of the practice of education.

In Chapter 1 I discuss the different roles that theory plays in research and make a case for beginning the discussion about theoretical frameworks or research paradigms more generally with the question of what the research seeks to achieve in terms of explanation, understanding, emancipation or a particular combination of such ambitions. I also engage with the most fundamental question about research: Why to engage with it at all? Chapter 2 focuses on the question of the improvement of education which, in my view, is an important ambition for all educational research. Against a tendency to think that improvement is about increasing the effectiveness of educational action, I argue that any claim to improvement has to begin with a discussion about the aims and purposes of education itself. I also suggest that improvement has a 'price', financially and educationally, and that research needs to take this into consideration as well. In Chapter 3 I extend this discussion with regard to recent calls to make educational practice evidence based by generating knowledge about 'what works'. I raise questions about the view of knowledge expressed in this ambition, the way in which the dynamics of educational practice are understood and the assumptions about the connection between research and practice, highlighting different ways for making educational research meaningful for the practice of education.

In Chapter 4 I zoom in on the question of what a practice actually is and why and how education might benefit from a practical rather than a theoretical 'framing'. Understanding education as practice and as a practice highlights that in the domain of education we are always working with *possible* relationships between actions and consequences, not with certainties. This means that educational practices require judgement about how to do things and about what is to be done. Such judgements are not just the 'work' of teachers and other educational practitioners, but have a public dimension as well, which begins to reveal connections between education, research and democracy. If Chapter 4 looks in a more formal sense at what a practice such as education is, Chapter 5 focuses more explicitly on what makes a practice *educational*. This question is explored in the context of the development of education as an academic discipline or field of study, comparing how this field has developed in the English-speaking world and in the German-speaking world. An awareness of such different 'configurations' of educational research is at least important in order to see that the way in which education and educational research are conceived in the English-speaking world is not the only way in which education and its research can exist.

Educational research that seeks to contribute to the improvement of educational practice needs, in some way, find a connection with educational practitioners, as they are central to the practice and the practising of education. In Chapter 6 I discuss this issue by means of an exploration of the ways in which educational research has either enhanced or limited the possibilities for educational professionals to judge and act. An awareness of these dynamics, and particularly the question to what extent research is part of the 'solution' or part of the 'problem', is important for any research that seeks to contribute to making education better. In Chapter 7 I bring these considerations to the topic of knowledge, particularly in order to explore what kind of ideas about knowledge would fit with the thoroughly practical nature of education and what such a 'fitting' way of understanding knowledge means for the claims research can make. In Chapter 8 I turn to questions about academic publishing, highlighting that publishing is no longer simply the way in which to share one's research findings with the wider world, but has actually become a complex global 'business' that is also interfering with research itself and with the ways in which research impacts on the wider world of education. I conclude the book with a brief epilogue in which I ask how much research education actually needs and whether less research might sometimes be better than more.

As mentioned, the chapters in this book do not constitute a systematic overview of what educational research is or how it should be conducted. They are rather meant to ask additional questions, open up different perspectives and perhaps provide the kind of orientation that may not immediately be there when one engages with educational research just through its orthodox (re)presentation. There is a certain order in the chapters, but they can also be read separately, ideally alongside other literature, in order to generate questions about and gain a perspective on educational research, its ambitions and limitations. At the end of each chapter there are five questions that may help with this.

Finally, I do not claim to have offered the last word about research, and also not the first, as I do think that it makes sense to start with the orthodoxies. I also do not want to close down discussion, but rather open it up. In this regard the ideas presented in this book might best be understood as what in German are called *Denkanstösse*: invitations for thinking and perhaps even provocations for thinking. My main ambition with all this is to make the conduct of educational research a little less orthodox and the work of researchers a little more intelligent, as John Dewey would put it.

1

Theories, Fashions and the Need for Pragmatism

At some point in the research process the question of theory emerges. Sometimes this happens early on, when researchers are looking for meaningful 'frames' for their research. Sometimes it happens 'midway', when researchers meet the challenge of how to 'make sense' of the data they have collected. And sometimes it occurs towards the end, when the question arises what the meaning of everything that has been found or constructed actually is. Theory is, therefore, an indispensable and inevitable part of research. But it is easy to get lost in the many theories and philosophies that are available. This chapter addresses this problem by means of an argument for pragmatism or, to be more precise, an argument for being pragmatic. Being pragmatic means nothing more than that any search for answers should always begin with posing a question, particularly the question 'What is the problem?' Such a pragmatic way of proceeding can help to keep control over the research process, and not let it be directed by theories, particularly not by the latest theoretical 'fashions'. Being pragmatic is also helpful in staying away from 'confessional' forms of engagement with theory, where researchers feel forced to confess themselves to a particular theory or theoretical position, rather than asking first what theory is actually supposed to do in and for their research.

Introduction: Being lost in other people's theories

I recently had the privilege of being the external examiner for five PhDs in education. The PhDs were written in different languages and emerged out of quite different academic cultures and traditions. The reason I was invited as external examiner most likely had to do with the fact that each of the PhDs made extensive use of theory, including some of the theory I have engaged with in my own work. What struck me was that all of these PhDs struggled with a similar issue, namely what to do with theory. In some cases, as I put it in one of my reports, it looked as if the authors had got a little lost in other people's theories.

The struggle with giving theory a proper place in one's research is not only a common problem in PhD projects but also an issue in the work of more experienced researchers, which often has a tendency either to be significantly *under*theorized or, like some of the PhD projects I examined, to be significantly *over*theorized (see Biesta, Allan & Edwards 2011). The question this raises is how one can find the right balance in engaging with theory in educational and social research. And this is a particular challenge in a time in which there seems to be a real proliferation of theory from such different disciplines and fields as philosophy, sociology, psychology, anthropology, social theory, political theory, cultural studies, feminism, post-colonialism, indigenous studies and so on, both at the level of 'object theory' – the theory we use *in* research – and with regard to 'meta-theory' – the theories *about* research.

The question here is not only about which theory or theories one should use to inform one's research but also about what one expects or hopes theory will 'do' in one's research. And perhaps there is even a bigger question as to why one should engage in research at all. In this chapter I wish to make an explicit case for pragmatism in the engagement with theory in educational and social research. This does *not* mean that I will express a preference for pragmatism as a theory or a philosophical position – to believe in pragmatism is actually the most unpragmatic thing one can do (see Biesta 2009a) – but rather that I will suggest that questions about theory in research should always be approached in a pragmatic way, that is, in connection to the question 'What is the problem?' – or, to be more precise: 'What is the question to which theory is supposed to provide the answer?'

On fashions, confessions and 'con-fashions'

The pragmatic approach I am advocating in this chapter can be distinguished from what we might term a *confessional* approach to the role of theory, one where the first step would be to 'sign up' to a particular theory or theoretical 'school' in order then to start doing the research. Such position-taking often takes the form of a kind of confession, such as in statements like 'I am a qualitative researcher' or 'I am a post-structural feminist'. While it is true that one can never start from nowhere and that in this regard there may be some sense in laying one's cards on the table, this shouldn't mean that one should do this in a confessional way, that is, as a matter of literally *taking* the position.

One important reason for this has to do with the fact that theories and philosophies are not so much positions one can 'occupy' as that they allow us to do certain things. Although the metaphor of 'tool' has become a little stale, it remains useful to see theories and philosophies as tools we work with, rather than as positions we take. Seen in this way it becomes visible what the problem is with confessing oneself to a theory. The first judgement, after all, is never about which tool one should use, but about what the issues are that need addressing, as it is only then that we can begin to ask which tool might be useful for addressing the issues. To compare it with carpentry, while a hammer can be a very appropriate tool for some tasks, it is entirely useless for other tasks, which shows that confessing oneself as being a *hammering* carpenter would seriously limit one's ability at being a *good* carpenter.

A further problem with a confessional approach has to do with the fact that if one thinks of theory and philosophy as something one can confess to, one immediately objectifies theory and philosophy and forgets that many and perhaps all of the theories and philosophies that are around – many of which, over time, have turned into identifiable 'positions' – were actually developed in order to address very particular problems. To disconnect theories and philosophies from the context in which they were developed and in which they were meaningful, runs the risk of making them into a 'thing' rather than seeing them as the specific outcomes of very specific processes. While the objectification of theory and philosophy can be a useful way to 'map' a particular field or to make sense of the different 'moves' within a particular discussion, it ultimately disconnects the 'product' from the 'process' and thus hinders the intelligent use of theory and philosophy.

The case for pragmatism therefore always comes with the suggestion that any theory, philosophy or theoretical or philosophical position one encounters should be (re)connected with the particular context in which it emerged and, more importantly, with the particular problems those working on the theory or philosophy sought to address. It comes, in more plain language, with the duty to understand the history or origin of the tools one encounters, so as to be able to make intelligent use of them.[1] It then becomes possible to see, for example, that the now often demonized split between mind and body that can be found in the work of René Descartes was not a matter of taking a particular position or articulating a particular theory about the mind and the body. Rather the idea emerged in the context of a much more complicated and much more urgent discussion about the question of human freedom and human responsibility in a situation in which modern science was pushing a picture of the universe as mechanistic and operating on deterministic laws of cause and effect. While one may disagree with the particular solution Descartes sought for safeguarding a space for human freedom and human responsibility, one can at least begin to appreciate why a split between mind and body provided a possible and quite meaningful response to those issues.

Similarly, while it has become fashionable to criticize the Kantian idea of 'rational autonomy' as too rational, too autonomous, too self-sufficient, too disconnected and, perhaps even, too male, his was an attempt to articulate the qualities a person would need at a time when European monarchies came to an end and questions about what it would mean to be a citizen emerged within the context of newly developing democratic societies. Rather than being obedient to the monarch, such citizens needed to be able to make up their own mind. Also, while the work of Vygotskij has become popular in many quarters, we should not think of his endeavour as an attempt to develop and defend 'a sociocultural position', but rather as an attempt at answering the question of the role of social interaction in the development of higher mental functioning.

To look pragmatically at theory – which thus requires to ask the question of what a particular theory or philosophy was developed *for*, which means to trace it back to the context in which it was developed and to reconnect it to the particular problems that those working on the development of the particular theory or philosophy sought to address – is even more important in those cases where theorists themselves begin to forget what it was that motivated their work in the first place. A recent example of this tendency

---

[1] Richard Rorty's 1979 book *Philosophy and the Mirror of Nature* is, for me, still a prime example of such a pragmatic reading of the history of modern philosophy and modern thought more generally. The same 'flavour' can be found in some of the key texts written by John Dewey, such as his *Reconstruction in Philosophy* (1920) and *The Quest for Certainty* (1929).

can be found in what is now often referred to as 'actor-network theory' or 'ANT'. This 'theory' originated in the context of an attempt to provide a non-sociological understanding of asymmetries in power and an influence in science and technology in order to overcome the problem that sociological analyses always ended up having to claim superior insights in the workings of science and technology (see Latour 1987). Yet over time, and partly also through the adoption by others of the insights developed in this context, ANT lost its connection with its context of origin and in a sense became the very kind of sociological theory that it sought to replace (see, for example, Law & Hassard 1999; Latour 2005).

Problems with being non-pragmatic

There are, therefore, a number of problems with a non-pragmatic engagement with and use of theory and philosophy in research. One is that if we disconnect a particular theory or philosophy from its context of origin, we end up giving it a status it never sought to have. Doing so runs the risk of putting us in a position in which we use *theory-as-truth* rather than *as-a-specific-answer -to-a-specific-question,* which, by the way, is a more precise and more specific approach than the idea of theory as a 'lens' or 'perspective'. It really is about reconnecting theory-as-answer to the question the theory was an answer *to*.

The risk of a non-pragmatic engagement with theory – theory as a position one confesses to – is also that it makes us susceptible to theoretical fashions without being able to provide a rationale and justification for the particular theory or philosophy we use. In this regard it is at least remarkable that so many research projects in education, not least PhD projects, have, over the past two decades or so, opted for 'a sociocultural perspective', while, more recently, suddenly everyone seems to be taking an 'affective' approach, or a 'post-human' or 'new materialist' one, often without having even the faintest idea about the complexities of 'old' materialism or all the important reasons and subtle debates under the heading of 'humanism'.

Operating in a non-pragmatic way not only makes it more difficult to actually justify one's selection but at the very same time pushes us in the direction of a confessional approach – and here it is also important to keep in mind that PhD students are often pushed or even forced in the direction of such a theoretical confession by more experienced researchers who have located themselves within a particular position, rather than that they operate pragmatically – a phenomenon that can particularly be found in the language of 'research paradigms'. A non-pragmatic stance with regard to theory thus leads to a situation where theory has control over us, rather than where we have control over the theory or theories we decide to use. That, once more, shows how a non-pragmatic approach prevents us from engaging with theory and philosophy in our research in an *intelligent* way.[2]

Theory, the very idea

Although the word 'theory' is easily used – and, so far, I have used it myself in a rather loose way – it is not entirely easy to identify what it refers to, not in the least because the meaning of the word has shifted significantly over time. If we go back to the Greek origins of the word – which, of course, always raises the further question where the Greeks got their words from – theory (θεωρία) had to do with spectatorship: being a spectator of a performance or a festival, including religious festivals; being an official envoy to a festival; consulting an oracle or making a journey in order to study something. Here we can see that the meaning of theory is firmly located within the domain of the empirical, as it is about direct experience and witnessing. With Plato and Aristotle, however, theory (θεωρία) became connected to the domain of the *non*-empirical, that is, of Platonic forms and Aristotelian universals. Theory (θεωρία) thus became understood as knowledge of a permanent and unchangeable reality 'behind' the empirical world of change, flux and appearances.

The distinction between empirical and theoretical knowledge gained further prominence with the rise of the world view of modern science in which the main role of theory became that of the *explanation* of causal connections between empirical phenomena. The need for theory had to do with the insight that while correlations between phenomena can be perceived, underlying causal connections are invisible. Theory was therefore needed to account for or speculate about underlying processes and mechanisms. Here

---

[2] The idea of 'intelligence' used here takes inspiration from John Dewey's idea of the transformation of 'trial-and-error' action into intelligent action (see, for example, Dewey 1938; Biesta & Burbules 2003).

theory transformed into what Gaston Bachelard (1986, p. 38) has called 'a science of the hidden'.

With the rise of hermeneutics and interpretivism in the late nineteenth century, theory also become a device for *understanding*, that is, for making intelligible *why* people say what they say and do what they do. The role of theory here is that of deepening and broadening everyday interpretations and experiences. The primary interest of *critical* theory, developed by the philosophers of the Frankfurt School working in a tradition going back to Marx, lied in exposing how hidden power structures influence and distort such experiences and interpretations. The ambition here is that the exposure of the workings of power can contribute to *emancipation* (see Carr & Kemmis 1986; Biesta 2010a).

The shift from theory as empirical to theory as *non*-empirical hints at one of the key roles theory plays in contemporary research, namely its role in the analysis and interpretation of empirical data. But while theory plays a crucial role in making data 'intelligible', it is important to see that theory does not just come at the very end of the research – when all the data have been collected – but also plays an important role in the initial phases of research. Here theory is crucial for the *conceptualization of the phenomenon* one wishes to investigate. For example, while a researcher may wish to study 'learning', it is only after one has engaged with the question of how one wishes to conceptualize learning – for example, as information processing, as behavioural change, as acquisition, as participation, as social practice and so on – that one can make decisions about which phenomena one should focus on and also *how* one might go about doing so (which are questions of research design, research methodology and methods for data collection).

Some researchers, more often those working at the interpretative end of the spectrum, reject the idea that theory should play such a role in the initial stages of the research, as they feel that this biases the research findings and blinds researchers from seeing aspects that fall outside of one's theoretical 'frame'. While it is, of course, always important to be open in research, this particular objection fails to see that the world never appears unconceptualized and untheorized, which means that *not* to engage with conceptualization runs the risk of uncritically accepting existing definitions and conceptions of the phenomenon under study. It also shouldn't be forgotten that to conceptualize learning as, for example, participation in no way fixes or predetermines what it is that one will find through empirical investigation about such participatory processes – which means, to put it in a more positive way, that the role theory plays in the initial stages of research can never *replace* empirical work.

Theory *of* educational and social research: Paradigms or purposes?

If the discussion so far has focused on the role theory plays *within* research, I now wish to move to a different aspect of the role of theory in research and a different dimension of the case for pragmatism. This has to do with the wider justification of particular approaches to research – sometimes referred to as the question of research philosophy but more often, particularly in the English-speaking world, as the question of *research paradigms*.[3] The language of research paradigms often suggests that there are a number of fundamentally different approaches to doing research, often labelled as 'quantitative' and 'qualitative' with, in some cases, a critical approach identified as a third research paradigm. A major problem with identifying different approaches to research in terms of 'quantitative' and 'qualitative' is that strictly speaking the labels 'quantitative' and 'qualitative' can only be applied to the kind of *data* one works with – either quantities or qualities, that is, either numbers or words/ concepts – but not to what one *does* with such data (see also Biesta 2010b).

Here one already needs to shift to different concepts, for example in terms of a distinction between research that 'quantifies' and, with a move that is actually difficult to express in the English language, research that 'qualifies'. Yet even such terms only refer to the way in which research 'works' with data, but doesn't provide any insight into what it is that the research is actually aiming for. Yet it is the latter question – the question of the particular *purpose*

---

[3]   One important source for a depiction of educational and social research in terms of paradigms is the chapter by Guba and Lincoln in the first edition of the *Handbook of Qualitative Research* (Guba and Lincoln 1994). Although Guba and Lincoln paint a more complex picture about research paradigms than the distinction between a quantitative, a qualitative and a critical paradigm, the discussion about research paradigms more often than not just proceeds in terms of these categories or even only in terms of quantitative versus qualitative. This uptake has also been reinforced by recent work on mixed methods in educational and social research, which often depicts different ways of mixing in terms of various combinations of quantitative and qualitative research (see, for example, Tashakkori & Teddlie 2010; and, for a critique, Biesta 2010b).

(or purposes) of research – that can help to see significant differences between differing research approaches. It is such a characterization – that is in terms of what research seeks to achieve – that I wish to identify as a pragmatic way of understanding the differences between research approaches. And the reason for calling it pragmatic is that it allows for the selection of a particular approach – particular data, a particular design, a particular methodology – on the basis of a considered judgement about what it is that one aims to achieve with one's research. This is in contrast to the confessional way where one would locate oneself within a particular paradigm without asking first for what reasons and purposes one would want to be located there. So how might we understand the different purposes of research? And what is implied by a choice for one option – which in a sense is always a choice *against* other options?

As I have briefly indicated earlier, in terms of what research aims to achieve, we can make a distinction between three distinctively different purposes: *explanation, understanding* and *emancipation.* The idea that the task of research is to explain has its roots in the natural sciences where explanation is generally understood in causal terms, that is, as the identification of connections between causes and effects – and in 'strong' interpretations of causality, as *necessary* connections between causes and effects; a way of thinking we can find, for example, in the idea of laws of nature. The ambition behind explanatory research is that once we are able to identify necessary connections between causes and effects – that is, once we are able to generate perfect *explanations* – we are, in principle, in a position to *predict* future events based on what is happening currently and, to the extent to which the causes can be manipulated, we are also able to *control* future events.

The idea of explanation – and perhaps we might add, the ambition of explanation – rests on particular assumptions about reality, namely that reality itself is 'made up' of causal connections between events. Such an ontology emerged in the wake of what is often termed the 'scientific revolution', that is, the rise of a mechanical world view which assumes that reality operates as a perfect clockwork. While it might be possible to *model* some events in physical reality in terms of perfect causal connections, it is not an assumption that can be held for the whole of physical reality – for example, at a subatomic level such strong causality is not a plausible assumption, and also many biological processes do not operate in such a mechanistic-causal way, something which has been theorized, for example, in complexity theory.

A more important question for educational and social research is whether human phenomena such as education can be approached in the same way, that is, whether it is plausible to assume that in the domain of human action we can also find strong connections between causes and effects. This question goes back to a much wider and older discussion which is often framed in terms of the question whether human action is *caused* or *motivated*, that is, whether human beings ultimately act as stimulus-response machines or whether they act on the basis of their interpretation of the situation, driven by their motivations for action. The latter view, which we can, for example, find in the work of Wilhelm Dilthey (1833–1911), argues that in the domain of human action we should not use a language of *causes* but rather a language of *reasons*.

This suggests the need for not only a different methodology for research that aims to take this reality seriously but also and first of all a different *purpose* for research. This is not that of aiming to explain underlying causal connections but rather that of trying to understand the reasons that govern human action. If under the aegis of explanation the role of theory is to make plausible why particular events take place in cause-effects-chains, then the role of theory in research that aims at understanding human action is to make plausible why people act as they act, first and foremost through reconstructions of people's perspectives and interpretations.[4]

Some see the difference between explanation and understanding basically as a difference at the level of *ontology* – that is, at the level of the assumptions we hold about the nature of the reality we are investigating. In that case the choice for either explanatory or interpretative research is a choice based on what one believes that the nature of social reality is. Others treat the question first and foremost as a *methodological* one; that is, to the extent to which social reality can function in a causal way it makes sense to aim for explanation and to the extent to which social reality cannot function in that way – or cannot be *made* to function in this way – research should aim at understanding. I am inclined to favour the second approach, partly because I do not think that physical reality simply works in a (strong) causal way and partly because

---

[4] An older but still really interesting discussion of the role of explanation and understanding in social research can be found in Hollis (1994). In this book Hollis also provides a very useful discussion of both 'individualistic' and 'holistic' conceptions of explanation and understanding, thus being able to combine accounts of both approaches (individualistic explanation, holistic explanation, individualistic understanding, holistic understanding) within psychology and sociology and related fields of research and scholarship.

I believe that social reality can be made to function in a causal way – which requires a particular intervention to which elsewhere I have referred as that of complexity reduction (see Biesta 2010c). The idea of complexity reduction – which I will discuss in more detail in the next chapter – shows, on the one hand, how open systems such as education can be made to behave in a more deterministic way and, on the other hand – and this is crucial – what the 'price' is that needs to be paid for making social systems work in a causal way.

The idea that the purpose of social and educational research should be to generate understanding of the experiences, interpretations and motivations of actors in order to make plausible why they act in the way they do, does, however, raise one further important question, which is whether the account people give of their own actions, perceptions and motivations can be taken as a true or correct account of what is going on. It is here that Marxist philosophy and theory has raised the possibility that our understandings can actually be *distorted* as a result of the way in which social power structures influence our understandings and interpretations. This is the problem of ideology, where ideological thought is thought that is not just socially determined – that is, thought that is 'produced' by social forces – but that, in the words of Karl Marx, 'denies this determination' (Marx, quoted in Eagleton 2007, p. 80).

If this is the case, if social actors are unable to perceive how their thoughts are determined by social power structure, then it means that the understanding actors have of their own situation is by definition inaccurate or 'false', and thus needs a different 'intervention' from research. This is not an intervention where research tries to clarify and systematize what actors already know about their situation, but where researchers make visible *to* social actors how their interpretations have been determined by underlying power structures and how the influence of such structure *distorts* their understanding of what is really going on in their lives. Making this visible allows social actors to become liberated from the ways in which power structures determine their thinking, which is why research that makes such a contribution is seen as orientated towards *emancipation* (for the field of education, see the still excellent discussion in Carr & Kemmis 1986).

While there is much more to say about the different purposes of social and educational research, thinking of different research approaches first and foremost in terms of their *purposes* – that is in terms of what they seek to achieve – rather than in terms of the kind of data that are being used, allows for a much more intelligent way to make decisions about the particular approach one should adopt. To look at different research approaches or 'paradigms' in terms of their purposes does allow for pragmatism, because the first question that researchers ask if they follow this approach is not what kind of data they should collect but what they seek to achieve with their research – whether they seek to explain, to generate understanding or to bring about emancipation.

Three options or an integrative view?

If the foregoing provides a different way to engage with the plurality of approaches available to social and educational researchers, there still is the question whether we should think of these approaches as separate – so that at some point there is still the need to commit oneself to one of them – or whether the approaches might actually be thought of as being in connection to each other. The latter view has been espoused by Jürgen Habermas, most notably in his books *Erkenntnis und Interesse* (Habermas 1968; translated as *Knowledge and Human Interests* and published in 1971) and *Zur Logik der Sozialwissenschaften* (Habermas 1970; translated as *On the Logic of the Social Sciences* and published in 1990). Rather than to think of explanation, understanding and emancipation as three different and separate 'modes' of research, Habermas suggests that explanation has a role to play in social research, but that when such research operates *exclusively* in an explanatory mode, it misrepresents the specific nature of social reality. (This misrepresentation can, in turn, lead to a distortion of this reality.)

That is why explanation always needs to be embedded in research that aims for understanding, so that the interpretations of human actors can have 'control' over explanations generated about (parts of) their actions. Yet Habermas acknowledges the key insight from the critical tradition which is that the understandings social actors have of their own actions can be distorted by the workings of power. Hence interpretative research needs, in turn, to be embedded within modes of critical research that can make visible how power operates on people's interpretations so that ultimately the whole research effort can contribute to emancipation. For Habermas, the emancipatory ambition of social research is therefore not an approach that is different and separate from research aiming at explanation or understanding. He argues for a 'nested' model where explanation is nested within understanding and understanding is nested within critical forms of research, so that the encompassing research effort may contribute to emancipation.

The most difficult question: Why do research at all?

So far, I have made a case for a pragmatic engagement with theory *within* research and a pragmatic approach to different research approaches. I have, in other words, made a case for pragmatism with regard to theory *in* research and with regard to theory *of* research. While I do think that at both 'levels' such a pragmatic approach can provide researchers with guidance about what they want theory to do in their research, rather than that their theory drives the research or, even worse, researchers get lost in the complexity of theory, the discussion so far has relied on the assumption that research is, in itself, a good idea. But if we want to be thoroughly pragmatic, we not only should be able to justify our particular choices *within* our research efforts but also need to engage with the question of *why to do research at all* – at the very least in order not to forget that research is not something good or desirable in itself, but is a very particular way to respond to problems and issues. So, what might we say in response to this 'most difficult' question? Let me conclude with some reflections on this question.

The main thrust in arguments *for* research – particularly but not exclusively in the social domain – is of a utilitarian nature; that is, they highlight that the outcomes of research can be *useful*. Sometimes, and this is perhaps the most tempting way to argue for the usefulness of research, this is done by highlighting that research provides us with technical knowledge, that is, knowledge of how to do things, of how to solve a problem or of how to change a situation for the better. This rationale goes back to the old idea that (causal) explanation provides us not only with the tools of prediction but also with the tools of intervention and control.

The idea of 'control' is not necessarily a bad idea, as there are many areas of our lives where control over what occurs is desirable and beneficial. Of course, this is again something that is most prominent in our engagement with the physical world where increased opportunities for control can add to security and an overall increase in the quality of life – for example with regard to our health. But the example of health is already an interesting one, because it is obvious that health is not just a matter of technology and control but also has an important subjective dimension. There are very different definitions of what it means to lead a healthy life or be healthy, and technology can never override such definitions or define what health and happiness are or ought to be.

In our engagement with the physical world we now have at least several centuries of experience with technical knowledge and technology, and have been able to assess both the benefits and dangers of such knowledge – which is not to suggest, of course, that this discussion has been settled and that there are no problems left. The ongoing advance of technology in many areas of our lives continues to raise complex ethical and political questions. In the social and educational domain, the question of technology is a different one because, as I have suggested earlier, the assumption that what happens in the social and educational domain is similar to how things work in the physical domain – that is, in terms of causes and effects – is highly problematic.

While it might be possible to 'push' social and educational processes towards quasi-causal ways of operating – an issue I will discuss in more detail in Chapter 2 – this comes always at a price, and thus raises the question whether we are willing to pay such a price – which shows that ethical and political questions are not only intended for ethical committees or politicians but are also questions that researchers *themselves* should engage with. There are, therefore, ontological, methodological and ethico-political issues with regard to the ambition that research can and ought to generate technical knowledge about social and educational processes – which is why the ongoing, but in my view rather naive, call to researchers to generate knowledge about 'what works' remains highly problematic (see Biesta 2007; 2010d; see also Chapters 2 and 3 of this book).

The usefulness of research is, however, not confined to the generation of technical knowledge and technology. Much social and educational research actually provides us with different ways to see, understand and interpret the situations we work in. De Vries (1990) has suggested to refer to this as 'cultural knowledge' and connects this to a different way in which research can be relevant for social practices, which he calls the cultural role of research. By providing different understandings of social and educational realities, research can not only help those working in such situations to see things in a more precise manner but can also alert us to problems that we may not have encountered before. Along the cultural line, social and educational research can therefore also lay claim to usefulness, not because it simply provides us with opportunities for control but because it provides us with a wider range of possibilities for action, based on a wider range of understandings.

It is here that social and educational research would often like to position itself, not as a controlling technology but rather as an emancipatory one, that is, one that provides social and educational actors with more and better opportunities for their own judgement, decision-making and action. Perhaps we should refer to this rationale for research as 'soft' emancipation, in order to distinguish it from the stronger and more specific emancipatory claims that come out of critical traditions of social and educational research where the ambition is not simply to provide social and educational actors with more options for action but to reveal the hidden workings of power in order to emancipate social and educational actors, and through them the 'audiences' they serve, from those workings. But here some caution is needed, in order not to paint a picture that only looks at the potentially positive or beneficial effects of social and educational research. There are two points that are important here.

One is the point made by Michel Foucault, that knowledge should never simply be understood as the very 'thing' that can liberate us from the workings of power. This is partly because power is not simply negative and not just to be understood as limitation but also positive and actually quite important if we wish to make any chance for the better. But it is also because knowledge itself is not free from power – not only in the old adage that 'knowledge *is* power' but also in the sense that as soon as we (claim to) know something we also have opened up avenues for control and the limitation of opportunities for action. This is clearly a problem for educational research, not least for those modes of research that aim to provide understanding about educational realities and experiences.

After all, to generate detailed knowledge of how, for example, students operate strategically within the educational system or, to refer to another field, how adults navigate the complex landscape of lifelong learning is not only 'interesting' knowledge but also provides politicians and policy makers – and even educators – with new avenues for control that ultimately can block the very spaces for action and agency that such students or adults were able to create for themselves. Knowledge, to put it briefly, is therefore never just a liberating technology – at the very same time it can be (and often is) a disciplining technology (see Foucault 1970), which is one of the main reasons why we should be careful about just claiming the utility of research in the social and educational domain.

If this raises some questions about 'soft' emancipatory ambitions of research, the other important reminder has to do with stronger emancipatory ambitions, particularly those that claim that social research can reveal to social actors what they themselves cannot see or know about their social situation and, ultimately, about their own thoughts and feelings. Here the idea of a 'science of the hidden' re-emerges, and the fundamental question is whether emancipation should indeed be understood as the act where one person tells another person what he or she is really thinking and feeling, or whether to think of emancipation in these terms is actually the most unemancipatory intervention of all.

Paulo Freire already identified this problem when in his *Pedagogy of the Oppressed* (Freire 1970) he argued that emancipation cannot be brought about through banking education, as such a form of education leaves the power differential between the educator and the one to be educated in place. While Freire would see this as an argument for a process of mutual and reciprocal learning towards the development of critical consciousness of both the oppressor and the oppressed – so that both identities can be overcome at the same time – Jacques Rancière has articulated a different option by disconnecting the question of emancipation from the question of knowledge and by thinking of equality not as the outcome of emancipatory processes but rather as a different starting point from where to conduct our actions (see Biesta 2010a; and for what such a different starting point might look like in education, see Biesta 2010e, 2017a).

Conclusion: Being pragmatic without becoming a pragmatist

In this chapter I have tried to make a case for a pragmatic way of proceeding in educational and social research in response to a problem I encountered and continue to encounter in much research, often but not exclusively in research conducted by PhD candidates. The problem is that such research often gives me the impression that its authors are lost in other people's theories, and it is against this background that I have suggested that a pragmatic approach might help to regain some control over what we want theory to do in our research endeavours.

A pragmatic approach implies that in all cases we connect our judgements and decisions to the question 'What is the problem?' so that we do not end up making choices for particular 'answers' – or in the metaphor I have used throughout this chapter: choices for particular tools – without at least trying to identify what is the question that we are trying to address and what is the problem that we are trying to solve. I have suggested that such a pragmatic attitude is needed at three levels: (1) with regard to the theories we use *in* our research, (2) with regard to the theories we use *about* our research (3) and with regard to the wider justification of research in the first place. The pragmatic attitude I have advocated in this chapter is explicitly not an argument to adopt pragmatism as a philosophy or philosophical framework for research, not in the least because the suggestion that one should adopt a particular framework is precisely the way of thinking I have tried to challenge.

Five questions for discussion and further consideration

1. What would be your honest answer to the question of why you are doing research at all?
2. How would you characterize the overall ambition of your research in terms of explanation, understanding or emancipation?
3. Can you identify what theory is doing in your research?
4. Could insights from your research be used in ways that go against your own intentions?
5. Do you know in which context and with regard to which problems or issues the theory/theories you are using were developed?

2

Making Education Better

It seems as if everyone agrees that the key motivation for doing research in and on education is so as to make education better. But this is about as far as it goes, because as soon as one asks what it would actually mean to make education better, how such an ambition might be achieved, and how one might judge whether education has actually improved, opinions begin to differ. While making education better sounds like a laudable ambition, it is actually fraught with difficulties and it is important for beginning researchers – but also for more experienced ones – to be fully aware of these difficulties. In this chapter I discuss a number of issues that are particularly related to the suggestion that the contribution of research to the improvement of education should focus on increasing the effectiveness of education. I suggest that whether an increase in effectiveness counts as improvement crucially depends on what it is one seeks to achieve – the question of educational purpose. I also suggest that this requires a judgement about the 'costs' of increasing effectiveness. In addition to this there is the question whether increasing effectiveness is the only way in which research can be meaningful for educational practice, which brings me back to the distinction between a technical and a cultural role for educational research.

Introduction: Improving education through research

Ever since the establishment of the first professorship in education at the University of Halle in Germany in 1779, educators and educationalists have raised questions about the potential contribution of research to the improvement of educational practice. Ernst Christian Trapp, the first holder of this chair, not only devoted his inaugural lecture to what has become known as the theory–practice problem in education (see Trapp 1779) but also contributed to the discussion via other publications, including one with the rather contemporary sounding title: *On the Promotion of Effective Knowledge* (*Von der Beförderung der wirksamen Erkentniss*; Trapp 1778).

The suggestion that one of the key tasks of educational research lies in increasing the effectiveness of educational action has been a recurring theme in discussions about the role of research in education. Recent manifestations of this line of thinking can be found in the school effectiveness movement (see, for example, Townsend 2007) and in the suggestion that educational research should focus on generating evidence about 'what works' (see, for example, Thomas & Pring 2004; Biesta 2007; see also Chapter 3). A relatively recent attempt at bridging the gap between research and practice can be found in *TLRP's 10 Principles for Effective Pedagogy* (James & Pollard 2012a), which were formulated on the basis of research[1] conducted in the UK's Teaching and Learning Research Programme, 'the largest programme of educational research on teaching and learning that the UK has ever seen' (James & Pollard 2012b, p. 269).

In this chapter I wish to raise a number of questions about the idea of educational improvement and about the role research can and should play in it. I will use TLRP's ten principles to illustrate what I see as some of the common problems in discussions about research and improvement. I will start with a brief presentation of the principles and will then focus on three issues. The first has to do with the idea that educational improvement entails increasing the effectiveness of educational processes and practices. Here I will argue that any discussion about effectiveness always needs to be connected to wider considerations about the aims and purposes of education. The second point has to do with underlying assumptions about the dynamics of education – that is, with ideas about how education 'works' and how it can be made to 'work'. I show that much of the discussion about educational improvement relies on a quasi-causal conception of education where the task of research is seen as that of identifying key variables so that the overall process and, more specifically,

---

[1] Note that the principles were formulated on the basis of a review of a selection of projects conducted within the Teaching and Learning Research Programme, rather than on the outcomes and insights from all projects conducted (see James & Pollard 2012a, pp. 323–8). Work conducted with in TLRP on learning through the life course (see Biesta et al. 2011; Goodson et al. 2010) was, for example, not included (also not in Brown 2009; David et al. n.d.).

the relationship between 'inputs' and 'outcomes' can be controlled. In response to this I will suggest a different way of looking at how education works and can be made to work, for which I will make use of insights from systems theory and complexity theory. This connects to the third point I wish to make, which has to do with assumptions about the kind of knowledge research can and should generate in order to be of practical use for education. Here I will discuss in more detail the distinction between a technical and a cultural role for research in relation to practice, and will point at the limitations of a technical role for research in the improvement of education.

TLRP's ten principles for effective pedagogy

My aim with this chapter is not to provide a critical analysis of TLRP's ten principles as such but to use them as an example of recent thinking about the relationships between research and practice in education, specifically with regard to the idea of educational improvement. The principles themselves have their background in what James and Pollard (2012b, p. 277) refer to as 'the conceptual map that TLRP has developed to represent the scope of its interests with reference to teaching and learning' (for the actual map, see ibid., p. 278) and in work that was conducted within the programme aimed at synthesizing findings from individual projects (see ibid.). A first iteration of the principles was published in 2006 (James & Pollard 2006) when the principles were presented as ten 'evidence-informed principles for effective teaching and learning' (James & Pollard 2012b, p. 279). Eventually it was decided to group the principles under four headings: (1) educational values and purposes; (2) curriculum, pedagogy and assessment; (3) personal and social processes and relationships and (4) teachers and policies (see ibid.).

While in a number of iterations the principles were presented as principles 'of effective teaching and learning' (ibid.), in the final presentation they were articulated as 'principles for effective pedagogy' (see ibid.). James and Pollard provide four reasons for the shift from 'teaching and learning' to 'pedagogy'. They claim that the term 'pedagogy' is less 'academic jargon' than other phrases, that it is 'now more widely used by UK practitioners and policy makers' than it was at the start of the Teaching and Learning Research Programme, that '"pedagogy" expresses the *contingent relationship* between teaching and learning ... and does not treat teaching as something that can be considered separately from an understanding of how learners learn' and that most of the TLRP projects actually focused more on 'implications for teaching of what we know about learning, than it did on developing new knowledge about learning per se' (James & Pollard 2012b, p. 280; emphasis in original).[2]

While the use of the term 'pedagogy' thus seems to indicate a shift away from the language of 'teaching and learning', James and Pollard nonetheless quote Alexander's definition of pedagogy as 'the act of teaching together with its attendant discourse' (Alexander 2004, p. 11, quoted in James & Pollard 2012b, p. 280) and add that this definition 'fits well with the way TLRP came to understand pedagogy', thus giving the impression that 'pedagogy' first and foremost refers to *teaching*. In this sense the conception of 'pedagogy' used here 'still' (see Simon, 1981; Alexander, 2004) differs significantly from its Continental counterpart, an issue I will return to in Chapter 5.

Inspiration for formulating the outcomes of the review of TLRP projects in terms of principles came from the way in which the UK Assessment Reform Group had used this format to summarize 'evidence on effective "assessment for learning"' (James & Pollard 2012a, p. 279). The final formulation of the ten principles – listed on the TLRP website under the heading of 'TLRP's evidence-informed pedagogic principles' and in James and Pollard (2012b) as 'TLRP's 10 principles for effective pedagogy' is as follows:

1. **Effective pedagogy equips learners for life in its broadest sense.**
   Learning should aim to help individuals and groups to develop the intellectual, personal and social resources that will enable them to participate as active citizens, contribute to economic development and flourish as individuals in a diverse and changing society. This means adopting a broad conception of worthwhile learning outcomes and taking seriously issues of equity and social justice for all.

2. **Effective pedagogy engages with valued forms of knowledge.** Pedagogy should engage learners with the big ideas, key skills and processes, modes of discourse, ways of thinking and practising, attitudes and relationships, which are the most valued learning processes and outcomes in particular

---

[2] An important exception may have been the 'Learning Lives' project which, as mentioned, was not utilized in the formulation of TLRP's principles.

contexts. They need to understand what constitutes quality, standards and expertise in different settings.

3. **Effective pedagogy recognises the importance of prior experience and learning.** Pedagogy should take account of what the learner knows already in order for them, and those who support their learning, to plan their next steps. This includes building on prior learning but also taking account of the personal and cultural experiences of different groups of learners.

4. **Effective pedagogy requires learning to be scaffolded.** Teachers, trainers and all those, including peers, who support the learning of others, should provide activities, cultures and structures of intellectual, social and emotional support to help learners to move forward in their learning. When these supports are removed the learning needs to be secure.

5. **Effective pedagogy needs assessment to be congruent with learning.** Assessment should be designed and implemented with the goal of achieving maximum validity both in terms of learning outcomes and learning processes. It should help to advance learning as well as determine whether learning has occurred.

6. **Effective pedagogy promotes the active engagement of the learner.** A chief goal of learning should be the promotion of learners' independence and autonomy. This involves acquiring a repertoire of learning strategies and practices, developing positive learning dispositions, and having the will and confidence to become agents in their own learning.

7. **Effective pedagogy fosters both individual and social processes and outcomes.** Learners should be encouraged and helped to build relationships and communication with others for learning purposes, in order to assist the mutual construction of knowledge and enhance the achievements of individuals and groups. Consulting learners about their learning and giving them a voice is both an expectation and a right.

8. **Effective pedagogy recognises the significance of informal learning.** Informal learning, such as learning out of school or away from the workplace, should be recognised as at least as significant as formal learning and should therefore be valued and appropriately utilised in formal processes.

9. **Effective pedagogy depends on the learning of all those who support the learning of others.** The need for lecturers, teachers, trainers and

co-workers to learn continuously in order to develop their knowledge and skill, and adapt and develop their roles, especially through practice-based inquiry, should be recognised and supported.

10. **Effective pedagogy demands consistent policy frameworks with support for learning as their primary focus.** Organisational and system level policies need to recognise the fundamental importance of continual learning – for individual, team, organisational and system success – and be designed to create effective learning environments for all learners.

http://www.tlrp.org/themes/themes/tenprinciples.html (last accessed 10 October 2012)

Educational improvement: Effectiveness or change for the better?

The idea of 'effective pedagogy' suggests that educational improvement is a matter of increasing the effectiveness of educational processes and practices. Here we can already find a very common but also very fundamental problem in the discourse about educational improvement. This problem has to do with the fact that 'effectiveness' is a *process* value, that is, a value that says something about the ability of certain processes to 'produce' certain 'outcomes'. What is not part of the idea of effectiveness is a judgement about the desirability of those outcomes themselves. The crude way to make the point here is to say that there is both ineffective and effective torturing, and while one may wish to work hard to increase the effectiveness of the torturing methods one deploys, it doesn't make the outcome any better. Ineffective torturing is, in this regard, as morally reprehensible as effective torturing.

While in a general sense it may be desirable, therefore, to have *more* effective rather than *less* effective ways of working in education[3] – albeit that the multidimensional nature of educational purpose makes this matter a bit

---

[3] It is perhaps important to briefly mention that effectiveness should also be distinguished from efficiency. Effectiveness concerns the question whether a particular approach or strategy will bring about the desired results and outcomes and also whether one particular approach or strategy can do this more securely than another. Efficiency, on the other hand, does not focus on the 'whether' but on the 'how' in that it asks about the resources that need to be deployed to bring about a desired result or outcome, and it is interested in using such resources in the most optimal way possible.

more complicated (see below) – just to argue that an increase in effectiveness constitutes educational improvement, is a rather empty statement if we do not specify what it is that the activity aims to achieve. Given that 'effectiveness' is a process value, a key question to ask with regard to educational improvement should therefore be 'Effective for *what*?' (see Bogotch, Mirón & Biesta 2007), and given that what may be effective for one individual or group may not necessarily be effective for another individual or group, one may wish to add a second question: 'Effective for *whom*?' (see ibid.; see also Peterson 1979, for a short publication that shows that the point is an old but perhaps forgotten one). In most of the ten principles the connection with the question of purpose seems to be absent.

When we take another look at the principles 2 to 10 it is remarkable that *general and decontextualized* claims are being made about how education ought to proceed, without providing any pragmatic 'framing', that is, without providing any insight into what it is that effective pedagogy is supposed to bring about. For example, while in some cases and for some purposes it might indeed be a good idea to engage with valued forms of knowledge, there are other cases when this is precisely not how education should proceed. Sometimes because the orientation is not on knowledge – think, for example, of the education of skills – and sometimes because the point is precisely for students to understand that there is no such thing as 'most valued' knowledge in the abstract, since what is valued by some is not necessarily valued by others, or what is valuable in one context is not necessarily also valuable in another context.

Similarly, when sometimes it can be a good idea to recognize the importance of prior experience and learning by taking account of what the learner knows already and by building upon prior learning, there are other cases when a radical break with such learning is called for, for example when students have misconceptions that block them from making progress in understanding, or because students have learned and internalized something about themselves, for example, that they are not suited for successful participation in formal education – a common theme when the question of learning is looked at from a life course perspective (see Biesta et al. 2011; Goodson et al. 2010).

The more general point I am trying to make here is that whether any of the ten principles mentioned in the list are indeed examples of effective pedagogy can only be judged if there is clarity about the aims that one seeks to achieve.

In this regard it matters crucially that education is a teleological practice, that is, a practice that is not only *framed* by its purpose (in Greek: telos) but also actually *constituted* by its purpose; that is to say that without a sense of purpose, direction or orientation education simply doesn't exist. Educational action, in other words, always raises the question of what the action is *for*, what it seeks to achieve and so on. This does not mean that such aims can or should be totally determined in advance, because an educator can also decide to initiate processes that are entirely open with regard to their possible outcomes. It also doesn't mean that only teachers or parents should be 'allowed' to formulate what the aims of the educational activity ought to be – although it can be claimed that they have a responsibility in educational processes and relationships that is fundamentally different from the responsibility of students and children.

One could say that the ten principles actually address this issue through what is stated in the first principle, namely the suggestion that 'effective pedagogy equips learners for life in its broadest sense'. Leaving aside the rather odd formulation in terms of 'effective pedagogy' – this is much more a general statement about the educational endeavour as a whole – one could say that there is little that is problematic in the assumption that school education should equip students for life in its broadest sense, and one could even say that this statement is so broad that it actually gives very little if any direction to educational processes and practices. The way in which this general statement is operationalized reveals, however, that it is not entirely open, particularly because James and Pollard seem to have opted for a rather 'functional' view of what education is for. They approvingly identify 'three major strands of philosophical and political thinking on educational purposes' (James & Pollard 2012b, p. 276), namely '*economic productivity*', '*social cohesion*' and '*personal development*' (ibid., emphasis in original). Moreover, these three strands of thinking on educational purposes are rather specific and are connected to very particular educational and political ideologies, more those of the *homo economicus* than, say, the *homo democraticus*. One could, after all, ask why it is that 'effective pedagogy' should focus on economic productivity and not on sustainable and respectful engagement with limited natural and social resources; why it should focus on social cohesion and not on peaceful democratic coexistence or why it should focus on personal development, fulfilment and expression, and not on compassion, altruism and ethical engagement.

Yet even with this particular formulation of the educational values and purposes that are supposed to give direction to our educational endeavours, there are still a number of further problems. One is that the other nine principles remain disconnected from what is stated in principle 1. No attempt is made, for example, to show that scaffolding is in all cases the more effective way to educate for individual flourishing or economic productivity than, for example, self-directed study or discovery learning. Secondly, the values and purposes listed in the first principle lack justification and in this regard raise the deeper question whether school education should be seen as a function of society – or even more specifically, a function of the state or the current government – or whether education should also be informed and guided by purposes that lie outside of this scope. This question – which is the question of the autonomy of the educational 'sphere' – has been an ongoing topic of discussion in the educational literature at least since Rousseau and can be formulated as the question whether school education should indeed be a function of and functional to society or the state or whether education always also entails a 'duty to resist' as the French educationalist Philippe Meirieu formulates it (see Meirieu 2008). Thirdly, the TLRP principles seem to narrow the question of educational purpose down to a formulation of 'learning outcomes' (see James & Pollard 2012b, p. 282), forgetting that any formulation of such 'outcomes' as the desired *results* of education is contingent upon a formulation of educational purposes rather than that such outcomes can replace such purposes.

While the question of educational purpose is therefore indispensable in any discussion about educational improvement and effectiveness, I do not think that the discussion about the purpose(s) of education should be thought of exclusively in terms of the formulation of differing ideological positions. As I have argued elsewhere in more detail (Biesta, 2010f), it is possible to create greater clarity in such discussions about what good (rather than effective) education is, by acknowledging that education never functions in relation to only one purpose or set of purposes but that educational activity always operates in relation to a number of different domains of educational purpose. One way to understand what is at stake here is to start by looking at the different areas in which school education actually has an impact. With regard to this I have suggested that it is possible to make a distinction between three areas in which education tends to function. One is the area of *qualification*. This has to do with the ways in which, through education, students acquire knowledge, skills and dispositions that qualify them to do certain things – and the 'doing' can either be very precise and confined such as, for example, the ability to perform a mathematical operation or execute a practical skill, or be very broad, such as the ability to navigate a complex multicultural society successfully.

A second is the area of *socialization*. This has to do with the ways in which, through education, students become part of and gain orientation within existing traditions, cultures and ways of being and doing. Here we can think, for example, of the ways in which education – either deliberately or in more 'hidden' ways – reproduces particular societal and cultural configurations and identities, sometimes because this is what education aims to do and sometimes because of the ways in which education actually operates. But professional socialization, that is, the deliberate attempt to make students competent members of particular professional communities, is another example of this – as are particular forms of religious and moral education. In addition to these two areas in which education functions, I have suggested that education always also impacts on the person, either to make students more dependent on existing structures and practices or with the intention of making them more independent from such structures and practices – a line of thought that connects to education as a process of emancipation.

While qualification, socialization and what I have suggested to call 'subjectification' – that is, the process of becoming-a-subject – can be seen as three distinctive functions of education, that is, three ways in which most if not all education functions and has an impact, qualification, socialization and subjectification can also be seen as three potential purposes of education or, in order to acknowledge that there are important choices to be made with regard to each of them, as *three domains of educational purpose*. To think of the question of purposes in education in this way at least allows for more precision in the discussion. But for the particular focus of this chapter there is another important advantage of looking at the question of educational purpose in this way. This advantage stems from the fact that the three domains of educational purpose pull education in different directions. There is, in other words, no complete synergy between the three domains, but rather scope for tension and conflict. While, for example, competition might be a desirable 'driver' in the domain of qualification – one could argue, for example, that in a competitive environment students will achieve more – it is not necessarily a desirable value in the domain of socialization – if, for example, one wishes to promote a collaborative attitude – nor is it automatically a desirable orientation in the domain of subjectification if, that is, one wishes to promote the emergence of a *homo democraticus* rather than, say, a *homo economicus*.

I am inclined to believe that the multidimensional character of educational purpose – that is, the fact that education always operates in relation to a number of different 'domains' – is something that is specific for the practice of education. Unlike other human practices which are often constituted and framed by a single orientation – for example, medicine's orientation on (the promotion of) health or the legal system's orientation on (the promotion of) justice – the multidimensionality of educational purpose means that there is always a need for judgement about how to *balance* the different 'interests' that education seeks to promote, and in many cases this will be a question of 'trade-offs', that is, how much one is willing to 'give in' in relation to one domain in order to promote particular achievement in relation to another domain, for example a little less in the domain of qualification so that more can be done in the domain of subjectification.

The main point I wish to make in relation to this is that it creates a very specific problem for the question of 'effective pedagogy' and the question of educational effectiveness more generally, because it means that what may be effective in furthering progress in relation to one domain of purpose may not be effective in relation to another domain. The question of educational effectiveness is therefore not only about connecting particular educational strategies and ways of working to what it is that one aims to achieve – which is why 'effective pedagogy' remains a meaningless idea until one specifies what it is that the pedagogy ought to be effective for, that is, what it ought to effect. The additional difficulty is that education always operates in relation to (at least) three different domains of educational purpose, so that what is effective in relation to one domain may be ineffective in relation to another or may at least limit or hinder or obstruct the effectiveness of another domain. This indicates that judgement is needed not only with respect to the relationship between means and ends but also with respect to potential tensions and conflicts between ends.

Some try to address this particular problem by arguing that school education should actually focus only on qualification – and that matters of socialization and subjectification belong to the remit of parents, but not of teachers. We can see this tendency at the level of policy, particularly when very narrow qualification agendas are being put forward as the only thing that counts and ought to count in education. Whether such an artificial reduction of the function of schooling is de facto possible remains to be seen. One could argue, after all, that even schools that are entirely constructed in terms of qualification still perform a socializing and subjectivizing role, as they socialize their students into the idea that the only thing that counts in life is knowledge and skills and that the only valuable way of being human is through qualification.

My observations about the ten principles and the idea of 'effective pedagogy' can be summarized by saying that 'effectiveness' is never an educational good in itself but only becomes a meaningful idea in relation to views about the purpose(s) of education. In this sense I wish to argue that in the field of education no approach or way of working is desirable in itself, because everything depends on what it is that one aims to achieve. Whether education should be flexible, personalized, student-led or motivating, or whether it should be strict, structured, general, teacher-led or difficult, entirely depends on what it is that one aims to achieve. In this regard we could say that all judgements about educational processes and practices are entirely *pragmatic*; they are never about the desirability of such processes and practices in themselves but always in relation to what they are supposed to bring about.[4] While increasing the effectiveness of education may count as a limited and rather technical definition of educational improvement, any judgements about whether change counts as improvement ultimately have to be made in relation to the wider purposes that orient the activity. Given the multidimensional character of educational purpose, an additional difficulty is that what is effective in relation to one domain of purpose is not necessarily effective in relation to another domain of purpose. This makes it extremely difficult if not impossible to speak about increasing the effectiveness of education in a general sense. Anything one can say here ultimately has to be said in relation to specific domains of educational purpose.

---

[4] The proviso here is that the means of education should be morally acceptable – my argument is not one where the ends justify the means but where the desirability of means can ultimately only be decided in relation to the question of ends. A further proviso is that in education means and ends are internally connected, which is a theoretical way of saying that students learn as much from what we say as from what we do. The means of education are therefore not neutral with regard to the ends but have educative 'force' themselves (see, for example, Carr 1992).

All this suggests that the very idea of formulating principles of effective pedagogy in a general and abstract sense is fundamentally flawed. Does that imply that it is actually impossible to formulate any principles for educational practice? I do not believe that this is the case, but it is important that one approaches such a task in a pragmatic way, that is, in the form of 'if ... then' statements, such as, 'if one wishes to increase students' exam scores, then it is advisable to train students as much as possible on the specific tasks in which they will be examined', or 'if one wishes to teach for understanding, then it is advisable to provide students with many opportunities for application, reflection and discussion'. Such an approach to the formulation of research-informed principles for educational improvement goes back to the work of Lawrence Stenhouse and is captured in the idea of 'principles of procedure' (see Stenhouse 1975). Principles of procedure are driven by educational aims and purposes – that is, by statements about what is considered to be desirable – and *then* try to articulate the approaches and ways of working that are likely to make a positive contribution to achieving these.[5]

Making education work: Causality or complexity?

If the foregoing section gives an idea of the kind of questions that need to be raised in order to engage with the issue of educational improvement as different from the issue of just increasing the effectiveness of the educational 'operation', I now wish to turn to the question about the role or roles that research has to play in this. I will do this in two steps. In this section I will look at assumptions about the dynamics of educational processes and practices. In the next section I will ask what kind or kinds of knowledge we might expect from research in relation to this and what this entails for the usefulness of research vis-à-vis educational practice.

The assumption that seems to inform many discussions about education and its improvement is that education works in a kind of causal way, where, on the one end, there are 'input' variables such as teaching, curriculum, assessment and perhaps also such variables as student ability, material resources and wider policies, and, on the other end we find a more or less wide range of

---

[5]   A concrete example of this particular approach can be found in James and Biesta (2007, pp. 143–60).

learning outcomes. While many researchers and policy makers would concede that there is still much that we do not know about the possible connections between all the variables, and while many would also concede that there is a complicated web of possible connections between 'inputs' and 'outcomes', the general tendency seems to be that this is just a *practical* matter; that is, if we just conduct more research we will, eventually, be able to identify the factors that determine the production of certain learning outcomes[6] – or, to put it in another popular discourse, we will eventually be able to determine 'what works'. That the assumptions are (quasi-)causal can already be seen from the language that is being used, that is, a language of 'inputs' and 'outcomes', of 'working' and of 'production'. But it can also be noted from research that tries to identify those factors that 'make a difference' (see, for example, Hattie 2008).

TLRP's ten principles also seem to be informed by quasi-causal assumptions. This can be glanced not only from the central role of the idea of 'effectiveness' but also from the 'conceptual map' which basically consists of a number of input variables, a process space where we find curriculum, pedagogy and assessment, and all this feeding into 'learning outcomes' (see James & Pollard 2012b, p. 278). While James and Pollard stress that the TLRP research projects have not managed 'to make unequivocal claims about findings in terms of categorical knowledge or cause-effect relationships' (ibid., p. 277), and while they also apologize for the fact that since most projects were conducted in authentic settings it was it 'impossible to control all the variables operating at any one time' (ibid.), these statements precisely show that ideally they think of the dynamics of education in the quasi-causal way outlined above.

One problem with causal assumptions about education is that they have difficulty with giving a place to the agency of the actors involved in education and, more specifically, with their reflexive agency – that is, with the fact that teachers and students can think and can act on the basis of their thoughts, judgements and decisions. One could of course suggest that these are precisely the aspects that need to be brought under control if education is ever able to work properly, and there is indeed a tendency within research on school effectiveness that considers the reflexivity of teachers and students as a

---

[6] Fenstermacher (1986) has raised some very important issues with regard to the common assumption that the purpose of teaching is to 'bring about' learning and has, instead, argued that if teaching can promote or produce anything, we should rather think of it in terms of bringing about 'studenting'.

problem rather than as part of the reality of education. But one could also argue that the fact that education 'works' as a result of the acts of reflexive agents implies that we need to think differently about its operation, not as a quasi-causal mechanical reality that happens behind the backs of those involved but rather as a (complex) social reality constituted by the conscious acts of reflexive agents. In one sense this has to do with a rather old and pervasive discussion in the field of education and social research more generally, which is the question whether the object of such research can be likened to that of the physical sciences, or whether it has its own distinctive nature. This is, of course, an important discussion – one that, in my view, is all too often replaced by the far less interesting methodological discussion about so-called 'qualitative' and 'quantitative' research – but slightly too big for the purposes of this chapter. A helpful way to make some progress, however, is through the languages of systems theory and complexity theory.[7]

Systems theory helps us to see that the idea of education as a production process – a process of input, throughput and output – and thus as a quasi-causal and ultimately a *perfectly* causal process, only makes sense under very specific conditions. Such conditions can only be found in closed deterministic systems, that is, systems that do not suffer from any interference from the outside and where, internally, the elements that make up the system work in a strictly deterministic way – where a causes b, b causes c and so on. While some (but actually not that many) systems in physical reality may operate in this way, educational systems do not operate like this – which already indicates why it is problematic to have assumptions about (perfect) causality with regard to education. The reason for this lies in the fact that education systems are open, semiotic and recursive systems.

Education systems are *open* because the boundaries with the environment are never completely closed – children, for example, go home after school and are therefore subjected to many more 'variables' than just those that can be controlled by the school environment. Education systems are *semiotic* in that the interactions between teachers and students are not based on physical push and pull but on communication and interpretation – students trying to make sense of what teachers are saying and doing and, through this, to learn from

---

[7] I have discussed this in more detail in Biesta (2010c).

their teachers. And education systems are *recursive* in that the actions of the 'elements' in the system (i.e. teachers and students) feed back into the system and alter the direction in which the system will develop. The main reason for this lies in the fact that the 'elements' in the system are not stimulus-response machines but thinking and feeling beings who, based on their perceptions and interpretations, can choose to act in a range of different ways.

Looking at education in this way may raise the question of how education systems manage to work at all, since there are so many gaps, slippages and uncertainties. Given that research has been able to find correlations between 'inputs' and 'outcomes', the argument is also made, sometimes, that depicting education as an open, semiotic and recursive system must be mistaken because research actually shows that education can 'work' in quasi-causal ways. The response to this is threefold. The first point to bear in mind is that whereas it is possible to find correlations between variables of many open, semiotic and recursive systems, what this particular way of understanding the 'working' of educational systems shows is how such correlations are actually 'achieved', that is, that they are the result of people trying to make sense, trying to communicate, trying to teach and trying to be taught, rather than that they happen behind the backs of those involved.

The second point that follows from depicting education in the way I have done is that it helps to understand much better what actually needs to be done (and actually is done) in order to make open, semiotic and recursive systems operate in more predictable ways. The key principle here is that of *complexity reduction*, which is about reducing the number of 'options' for action available to the 'elements' in the system.[8] With regard to education systems, complexity reduction can be achieved along three lines: (1) through reducing the openness of the system; (2) through reducing the meaning-making (semiosis) that goes on within the system and (3) through reducing the recursivity of the system, either by blocking feedback loops or by stopping the 'elements' from acting in reflexive ways. When we look at education, we can actually see concrete examples of complexity reduction in order to make education 'work'. School buildings, curricula, timetables or home work are all attempts at reducing

---

[8] The way in which fast-food restaurants like McDonald's operate provides an excellent example of what it means to reduce the complexity of open, semiotic and recursive systems.

the openness of the education system by reducing the potential impact of influences from the outside. Assessment is one key way in which education reduces and tries to control meaning-making by making selections from all the possible interpretations that students generate and by identifying some as 'correct', 'right' or 'true' and others as 'wrong', 'mistaken' or 'false'. And many operational procedures – such as teachers' meetings, complaints procedures, as well as professional development – are all measures to reduce and control feedback loops.

In one sense there is nothing wrong with the reduction of the complexity of the education system as it is precisely through such measures that the system can work. But when we look at the ways in which education can be made to work in this way, we can begin to imagine that there is a tipping point where complexity reduction turns into unjustifiable control. This is the point where, for example, all interaction with the outside world is blocked, where students are being told that there is only one right answer and one proper way to behave, where teacher reflection and student reflection are taken out of the system and so on. The point here is that it is to a large extent possible to turn open social systems such as education into closed deterministic systems, but that this always comes at a price. So the key question is not whether we should try to reduce the complexity of the education system but *to what extent* we should be doing this, for what reasons and what the price is that we should be willing to pay for this. One critical 'tipping point', so I wish to suggest, concerns the moment where students can no longer appear as subjects of initiative and responsibility and are turned into objects of educational intervention. This is the point where education turns into indoctrination – the point where education itself comes to an end.

What do these observations mean for educational improvement and the role of research in it? I wish to suggest that if we approach the task of educational improvement in terms of a quasi-causal understanding of the dynamics of educational processes and practices, we are in a sense operating with a 'black box' conception of education where we assume some kind of (mysterious) connection between 'inputs' and 'outcomes' but have little idea of how such connections are actually achieved. This is why correlational research between 'inputs', 'outcomes' and 'mediating variables' *without* a proper theory of the underlying dynamics is actually of limited utility as it neither gives us an understanding of *how* such correlations are 'achieved' nor provides us with an understanding of the potential *drivers for educational change* towards improvement.[9]

While one can debate, of course, what would count as an appropriate theory, I have suggested that ideas from systems theory and complexity theory provide a rather helpful way to make sense of how education 'works' when we acknowledge that the main work for making education work is done by reflexive agents – teachers and students – not by mysterious (quasi-)causal powers.

3   The practical roles of research

The foregoing observations also have important implication for what we expect from research. In the discussion about educational improvement in terms of effectiveness and 'what works' one could say that the main if not only expectation there is about research is that it generates *technical* knowledge, that is, knowledge about possible relationships between variables – and in education the focus is perhaps first and foremost on the relationship between those variables that can be controlled by the teacher, which include pedagogy (in the narrow sense), curriculum and assessment. Technical knowledge, however, tends to rely on quasi-causal assumptions about the dynamics of education. While, as I have suggested, open, semiotic and recursive systems such as education can be pushed towards greater predictability by reducing the complexity of its operation, thinking of them in quasi-causal terms assumes a 'black box' approach that does not generate understanding about the actual dynamics at work. In this particular regard the quest for technical knowledge in education is problematic, perhaps first and foremost because such knowledge is in itself unable to provide insights into *why* things are actually working as they work. If we think of such knowledge and the research that generates such knowledge as part of a much wider attempt to reduce and ultimately control the complexity of the educational system, we can begin to see something of the politics of complexity reduction that operates through such a research-policy-practice 'complex'.

---

[9] I use the phrase 'change towards improvement' against the background of what I have said in the previous section about effectiveness and improvement.

One could see this as an argument for the need for a different kind of technical knowledge, and hence a different kind of research, one that actually probes deeper into the dynamics of educational systems. While in one sense this is indeed what follows from the line I have been pursuing in this chapter, to suggest that this is still a kind of technical knowledge misses an important point about the social ontology of education I have tried to articulate here, which is the fact that this particular social ontology assumes that education works as a result of the intentional activities of reflexive agents. This means that an important avenue for educational change towards improvement precisely is to be found in the ways in which the agents in the situation make sense of the situation and the activities going on inside it.

Just as knowledge about possible connections between actions and consequences might inform the perceptions, judgements and actions of educational agents, so do different conceptions and interpretations of what might be going on. It does, after all, make all the difference whether one sees a classroom in terms of behavioural objectives, learning difficulties, inclusion, legitimate peripheral participation, critical race theory or teaching as a gift – to name but a few different ways in which educational processes and practices can be made meaningful. The kind of knowledge that research can offer in relation to this – and I do take 'research' in the broad sense of including empirical and theoretical scholarship – can, as I have already mentioned in the previous chapter, be referred to as *cultural* knowledge (see De Vries 1990). This is knowledge that provides us with different interpretations of educational phenomena (including the important but difficult task as to what it means to 'name' a phenomenon as an educational one in the first place; see Chapter 5).

De Vries utilizes the distinction between these two 'modes' of knowledge to identify two different ways in which research can actually be of practical use, one to which he refers as the technical role of research and the other to which he refers as the cultural role. When research performs a technical role vis-à-vis educational practice, it provides technical knowledge, that is, knowledge about possible relationships between 'inputs' and 'outcomes' and, most importantly, about those 'inputs' that can in some way be controlled by teachers and other educational agents. When research performs a cultural role vis-à-vis educational practice it provides practice with different interpretations, different ways of meaning-making and different ways of sense-making.

The point De Vries makes – and this is in line with what I have been trying to argue in this chapter – is that along both lines research can contribute to the improvement of educational practices, which means that research can do more than just what is assumed in discussions about effectiveness and 'what works'. What I have tried to argue in addition to this is that the technical role is actually rather limited and that a more complex understanding of the dynamics of educational processes and practices actually hints at the need for different knowledge and understanding – particularly knowledge and understanding that take the role of reflexive intentional agents into account. The irony here is that whereas much educational research also in a strict technical 'mode' on the one hand assumes the existence of such reflexive intentional agents – otherwise, why would researchers bother to formulate principles for the improvement of educational practice – when such recommendations come in a technical form they imply at the very same time that education works behind the back of such reflexive intentional agents.

Although James and Pollard (2012b) concede that the TLRP projects have actually generated only a limited amount of technical knowledge it is therefore striking that the ten principles are mainly formulated on the basis of a quasi-causal understanding of education and on the idea that what the improvement of education requires first and foremost is technical knowledge about how to make the overall operation more effective.

Conclusions

In this chapter I have tried to raise a number of critical questions about educational improvement and the role research can play in it. I have used TLRP's ten principles for effective pedagogy as a 'case' for exploring these questions in more detail. I have argued that educational improvement cannot be understood as just an increase in the effectiveness of the educational operation but always needs to engage with the question of what education should be effective for, that is, with the question of educational purpose, as it is only in relation to this that a distinction between educational change and educational improvement can be made. I have suggested that the multidimensional nature of educational purpose puts a further limit on effectiveness thinking in that what might be an effective approach or strategy with regard to one (domain of) purpose may not be effective in relation to another (domain of) purpose.

This is why educational judgement is always required and research can never be translated into abstract and general principles for effective pedagogy.

In addition, I have shown that much talk about educational improvement relies on a quasi-causal conception of education which basically refrains from theorizing the dynamics of education and rather relies on a black box account that looks for correlations between 'inputs' and 'outcomes'. I have used insights from complexity and systems theory to open up this black box, particularly in order to acknowledge that education always involves reflexive intentional agents. I have shown how such a 'social ontology' of education not only opens up new avenues for educational improvement – avenues that always need to engage with normative questions about the price we are willing to pay for making educational systems more predictable. I have also suggested that this puts further limits on the possibility for generating technical knowledge about education and that at the very same time it provides us with a better understanding of the importance of what I have termed 'cultural knowledge' in relation to the improvement of education.

Do any lessons follow from this for where educational research might go if it is committed to the improvement of education? I think it does, but perhaps the main lesson to follow from it has to do with the urgent need to get a better understanding of education as a teleological practice – so that any questions about improvement are always dealt with pragmatically, that is, in relation to what it is that one aims to achieve through education – and also with an urgent need to get a better understanding of the dynamics of education, for which I have suggested the value of a complexity-informed understanding. This partly points at the need for more and better educational theory. And it points at the need to move beyond futile discussions about 'qualitative' versus 'quantitative' towards discussions that take their starting point in questions about the particular nature of educational processes and practices. The case of TLRP's ten principles for effective pedagogy shows that much of this is still lacking in 'the largest programme of educational research on teaching and learning that the UK has ever seen'.

Five questions for discussion and further consideration

1. In what ways does your research seek to contribute to the improvement of education?

2. How do your ideas about the improvement of education relate to the three domains (qualification, socialization and subjectification) of educational purpose?
3. What kind of (implicit or explicit) model of the dynamics of education underlies your research, and how does this compare to the idea of education as an open, semiotic and recursive system?
4. If your research results in suggestions for the improvement of education, have you also got something to say about the 'costs', financially, educationally or otherwise, of achieving such improvement?
5. Where does your research sit on the 'technical-cultural' spectrum, in terms of knowledge and its relationship with educational practice?

3

'What Works' Is Not Enough

It is easy to suggest that educational research should focus on 'what works', and it seems that it is almost impossible to contest this suggestion. The 'what works' mantra sounds tempting, but on closer inspection there are significant problems with the idea that research should generate knowledge about 'what works', with the suggestion that this can best be done through conducting large-scale randomized controlled trials and with the idea that all this will provide educational practice with a strong 'evidence base' that will contribute significantly to educational improvement. In this chapter I provide a critical discussion of some of the key assumptions of the idea that education should become an evidence-based profession and that knowledge about 'what works' can put education on this trajectory. In the discussion I highlight three deficits to which I refer as the knowledge deficit, the efficacy deficit and application deficit. Taking up some themes and insights from the previous two chapters, I conclude that education needs to be value based rather than evidence based because it is only on the basis of normative judgements about what good education is that the practice of education becomes possible. For precisely that reason any reference to 'what works' is simply not enough.

Introduction: Towards an evidence-based profession?

The idea that professional practices such as education should be based upon or at least be informed by evidence has become influential in many countries around the world (for an overview, see Wiseman 2010). A quick scan of journal titles not only indicates the growing popularity of the idea of evidence-based practice but also highlights its presence in a large number of professional domains, ranging from medicine – where the idea of evidence-based practice was initially developed in the early 1990s (see Guyatt et al. 1992) – via such areas as social work, mentoring and even library and information practice, through to education.[1] There is, of course, something intuitively appealing about the idea that evidence should play a role in professional work, and it is difficult to imagine an argument against engagement with evidence. This is even more so because professions, unlike other areas of work, lay claim to the possession of 'specialized knowledge and skill thought to be of value to human life' (Freidson 1994, p. 167). This not only raises general questions about the basis for the knowledge and skills professionals deploy. Given that professional work is generally orientated towards human well-being, there seems to be a prima facie case for basing professional action on the best knowledge available.

This is not to say that evidence should be the *only* thing that matters in professional practices. The important question, therefore, is not *whether or not* there should be a role for evidence in processional action, but what kind of role it should play (see also Otto, Polutta & Ziegler 2009). This at the very same time requires reflection on the question of what kind of role it *can* play, as there is no point in having expectations about evidence that are impossible to realize. The latter point is particularly important in relation to the uptake of the idea of evidence-based practice by policy makers, where there is a tendency to expect far too much from evidence (see, for example, Weiss et al. 2008). This becomes deeply problematic in those cases in which it is argued that professionals should *only* be allowed to do those things for which there is positive research evidence available – an approach which Holmes et al. (2006) have, in my view, correctly identified as a form of totalitarianism.[2]

The idea of evidence-based practice has generated a substantial amount of discussion between those who are generally in favour of giving evidence a more prominent place in professional practices and those who have raised concerns either about the idea of evidence-based practice in general or about

---

[1]   A (random) selection of journal titles devoted to the idea of evidence-based practice: *The Journal of Evidence-Based Medicine*, *The Journal of Evidence-Based Healthcare*, *The Journal of Evidence-based Dental Practice*, *Evidence Based Nursing*, *The Journal of Evidence-Based Social Work*, *Journal of Evidence Based Health Policy and Management*, *The International Journal of Evidence Based Coaching and Mentoring*, *The Journal of Evidence Based Library and Information Practice* and *The Journal of Evidence-Based Practices for Schools*.

[2]   Holmes et al. (2006) also use the notion of 'microfascism' to criticize the discourse on evidence within the health sciences and make a convincing case for the use of this notion.

its applicability in specific professional domains (see, for example, Hammersley 2005; Smeyers & Depaepe 2006; Holmes et al. 2006; Cornish & Gillespie 2009; St. Clair 2009). While some authors caution about what can be expected from scientific evidence, others continue to promote research that emulates 'the medical model' as the solution to many if not all problems in the field of education (for such a view, see Prenzel 2009; for an alternative see Biesta 2010g). In my own contributions to the discussion I have particularly highlighted the 'democratic deficit' of the uptake of the idea of evidence-based practice in education, emphasizing how a particular use of evidence threatens to *replace* professional judgement and the wider democratic deliberation about the aims and ends and the conduct of education (see Biesta 2007). In this chapter I will revisit some aspects of this earlier discussion and will add some further dimensions to the analysis. I will present my reflections in the form of a case for value-based education as an alternative for evidence-based education. Calling the idea of value-based education an alternative is not meant to suggest that evidence plays no role at all in value-based education but to highlight that its role is subordinate to the values that constitute practices as *educational* practices.

In my analysis I will focus on three aspects: epistemology, ontology and practice. In each case I will present two different 'readings' of the particular dimension. In the case of epistemology, I will make a distinction between representational and transactional epistemologies; in the case of ontology I will make a distinction between closed and open systems; in the case of practice I will make a distinction between application and incorporation. In all three cases I will identify a deficit. In the epistemological domain there is a *knowledge deficit*, in the ontological domain an *effectiveness* or *efficacy deficit* and in the practice domain an *application deficit*. Taken together these deficits not only raise some important questions about the very idea of evidence-based practice but also highlight the role of normativity, power and values. In the final section I will discuss the implications of these deficits for the practice of education which, in turn, will lead me to my case for value-based education. As I am generally worried about the expectations policy makers hold about what evidence can and should do in relation to professional practices such as education, my contribution is primarily meant to provide educators with insights and arguments that can help them to resist unwarranted expectations about the role of evidence in their practices and even more so of unwarranted interventions in their practices.

Evidence about 'what works'?

A useful starting point for the discussion of the idea of evidence-based practice can be found in the meaning of the word 'evidence' itself. The Oxford dictionary defines evidence as 'the available body of facts or information indicating whether a belief or proposition is true or valid'.[3] While evidence therefore has to do with the question of truth, it is important to see that under this definition it is not evidence itself to which the question of truth or falsity applies. If we define knowledge as 'justified true belief' – which implies that for someone to know something it must be true, it must be believed to be true and the belief must be justified – then evidence plays a crucial role in the *justification* of such beliefs.[4] Evidence, in other words, contributes to the case for holding a particular belief as true and in this regard its meaning is slightly different from that of the word 'knowledge'. This is not just semantic play – although it is interesting to ponder the different rhetorical effects of the notions of 'evidence-based practice' and 'knowledge-based practice' – but opens up the possibility that what counts as evidence can be broader than just true knowledge (think, for example, of the role of testimonies and witness reports in building up evidence in a court case). It also suggests that rather than there being a mechanistic connection between evidence and truth, there is a need for judgement about the relative weight of what is being submitted as evidence for a particular belief or proposition.

While all this may be so in theory, things tend to work out more crudely in practice (see also Hammersley 2009). In discussions about evidence-based practice, 'evidence' is often exclusively considered in cognitive terms, that is, as knowledge and, more specifically, as *true knowledge*. Evidence is further narrowed down to *scientific* knowledge understood as knowledge generated through scientific research. In effect the focus tends to be on one particular kind of scientific research, namely *experimental research* and, more specifically, the randomized control trial, as this is considered to be the only reliable way in which valid scientific knowledge about 'what works' can be

---

[3] *The Oxford Pocket Dictionary of Current English*. 2009. Retrieved September 15, 2009 from Encyclopedia.com: http://www.encyclopedia.com/doc/1O999-evidence.html.

[4] Whether it is possible to conceive of knowledge as 'justified true belief' is another matter. The issue has been a topic for discussion ever since Gettier (1963) provided examples of justified true beliefs that would not count as cases of knowledge.

generated. The emphasis on the idea of 'what works' is, in itself, relevant because of the fact that many if not all professions operate on the model of initiating change in order to bring about a situation that is considered to be better or more desirable. The question whether professional interventions will have the desired 'effect' is, therefore, a very important one, which explains why in discussions about evidence-based practice the 'what works' questions plays a central role.

There are, however, three issues that need to be considered in relation to this. The first issue – the *epistemological* dimension of the discussion – has to do with the question of how we can generate knowledge about 'what works' and, more specifically, how we should understand the status of knowledge generated through experimental research. The second issue – the *ontological* dimension of the discussion – has to do with the question of how links between interventions and effects are actually achieved and particularly how it is possible to make things work in the social domain. The third issue – the *practice* dimension of the discussion – has to do with the question as to what extent professional practice can actually be said to be based upon knowledge or evidence and whether we should understand the advance of evidence-based practice indeed in terms of the application of scientific knowledge.

Epistemology: Representation or transaction?

I have suggested that despite the more precise meaning that can be given to the notion of 'evidence', the evidence that is supposed to form the basis for practice is commonly seen as true scientific knowledge about 'what works' generated through the application of randomized controlled trials. One question this raises is how 'truth' should be understood in this context. Although relatively little attention has been paid to the epistemological dimensions of evidence-based practice, the discussion gives the impression that the case for evidence-based practices relies on a representational epistemology in which true knowledge is seen as an accurate representation of how 'things' are in 'the world'. If we are indeed able to generate true and complete knowledge about how things are in the world and about the laws that govern the connections between things, then it should at some point be possible to say with certainty that when we do A, B will follow. Viewed from this angle the fact that we do not yet have such knowledge in fields such as education is not a *structural* problem but a *practical* one: it indicates that we have not *yet* conducted sufficient research in order to be able to encapsulate all factors, aspects and dimensions that make up the reality of education. If we are able to coordinate our research efforts and channel available resources all in the same direction then, so the argument often goes (see, for example, Prenzel 2009), we will, at some point in time, have a perfect evidence base for educational practice – and, on the same logic, for any other field of practice.

I do not consider it very fruitful to engage in abstract discussions about whether true or objective or complete or perfect knowledge is possible or not, not in the least because in such discussions those who are in favour and those who argue against often base their arguments on a similar set of premises (see Bernstein 1983; Biesta & Burbules 2003; Biesta 2005). I rather wish to highlight a more practical point, which has to do with the tension between a representational epistemology and an experimental methodology.[5] Whereas a representational epistemology sees knowledge as a picture of a world independent from and unaffected by the knower – an idea which John Dewey has helpfully referred to as a 'spectator view' of knowledge – experimentation is always an *intervention* in that world. From a representational point of view such interventions can only be seen as distortions of the world, which implies that they pose a threat to the possibility to gain true knowledge.[6] The way out of this predicament is *not* to discredit the role of experimentation in the generation of knowledge – one could argue, after all, that most if not all of the knowledge that underlies modern technology has been generated through experimentation and intervention – but rather to investigate the implications for epistemology of an interventionist and experimental approach to the generation of knowledge. This is precisely the route taken by John Dewey in his writings on knowledge and knowing.

In Chapter 7 I will discuss Dewey's ideas in more detail (see also Biesta & Burbules 2003). Here I wish to highlight one important implication of Dewey's view – an implication that has important ramifications for the epistemological underpinnings of the idea of evidence-based practice. The point is that if we

---

[5] This is a very brief summary of a point made in much detail by John Dewey – see, for example, Dewey (1929).

[6] This is an issue that has also troubled the interpretation of quantum physics.

take experimentation seriously in our understanding of what knowledge is and how we can get it, we have to give up the spectator view of knowledge – the one which assumes that knowledge is about observing a static, observer-independent reality – and rather have to concede that the knowledge we can gain through experimentation is knowledge about *relationships* and, more specifically, about relationships between (our) actions and (their) consequences. In contrast to a *representational* epistemology we can call this a *transactional* epistemology (Biesta & Burbules 2003). In a transactional epistemology experimentation no longer appears as a distortion of reality but rather as an indispensable element of the way in which we gain knowledge about reality. Such knowledge is not a depiction of a static world 'out there' – in the traditional sense of the word such knowledge is not objective because we are involved in the production of it. Yet it also isn't knowledge just created by our minds – which means that in the traditional sense of the word it is also not subjective. It rather is knowledge about the world *in function of* our interventions. Taking experimentation seriously thus means that we have to give up the idea that it is possible to achieve complete knowledge about reality. This is not because our knowledge can always only be a subjective approximation of reality – the view espoused by Karl Popper – but because 'the world' always appears in function of our interventions and because 'the world' changes as a result of our interventions. Rather than being spectators of a finished universe, Dewey's pragmatism amounts to the idea that we are participants in an ever-evolving universe.

Dewey's transactional epistemology appears to suit the idea of 'what works' rather well. After all, the focus is entirely on relationships between actions and consequences, which suggests that the knowledge generated through experimentation can indeed tell us 'what works'. But there is a crucial difference between a reading of the notion of 'what works' in terms of a representational epistemology and in terms of a transactional epistemology. Whereas in terms of a representational epistemology knowledge about what works extends to the *future* – after all, if we have complete knowledge about reality as it is in itself, this knowledge should remain valid in the future – the transactional view implies that all we can know concerns relationships between actions and consequences that have occurred in the *past*. Whereas a representational epistemology would suggest that our knowledge provides us with *certainty*, a transactional epistemology – the one that can take experimentation seriously – can show us what has been *possible* in the past with *no guarantee that what has been possible in the past will also happen in the future.*

A transactional epistemology allows us to make warranted assertions about what *has worked* in the past but not about what *will work* in the future. Knowledge about what has worked in the past is, of course, tremendously important in our attempts to deal with problems in the here and now, as it can provide us with new and different ways to understand the problems we encounter in the here and now and because it can provide us with hypotheses for problem-solving in the present. It can make, in Dewey's words, our action and problem-solving more intelligent. But what evidence generated through experimentation cannot do on this account is provide us with rules for action and even less with dictates for action.[7] I wish to refer to this gap between the knowledge that can be generated through experimental research and the way in which this knowledge can be utilized as the *knowledge deficit* of evidence-based practice, indicating that there is *always* – structurally, not pragmatically – a gap between the knowledge we have and the situations in which we have to act. In this regard the so-called 'knowledge-base' for practice is never sufficient and never will be sufficient. This, in turn, raises the question of how this gap is closed in practice – something to which I will return below.

Ontology: Causality or complexity?

For the discussion about evidence-based practice there is not only the question whether it is possible to have perfect knowledge about the relationships between interventions and their effects; there is also the question about these relationships themselves. How do interventions work? How are links

---

[7] I wish to emphasize that the point I am making here does not rely on a claim for the alleged superiority of a transactional epistemology. Rather than seeing my point as a general philosophical one, it actually centres on the question of what follows if we apply an epistemology that can take experimentation seriously. The 'case' for a transactional epistemology is therefore only based on the attempt to overcome the tension – if not contradiction – between the experimental methodology that plays a central role in the ideas of proponents of evidence-based practice and the representational epistemology that they seem to employ in arguing for the alleged superiority of the knowledge generated in this way.

between actions and effects established? The simple – and by now we should actually say, simplistic – idea is to assume that interventions are causes and results effects, and that, under optimal conditions, the causes will *necessarily* generate the effects. This is a kind of 'magic bullet' notion of causality which, if possible at all in the social domain, actually only exists under very special conditions. As I have already discussed in detail in Chapter 2, such 'strong' causality only occurs in closed systems that operate in a linear deterministic way. Yet this is precisely what education is not; education is an open, semiotic and recursive system. It functions through meaning and interpretation rather than in a deterministic way, and it functions recursively rather than in a linear manner.

These ideas from systems theory and complexity theory are helpful, as mentioned, because they can highlight that whereas much talk about 'what works' is premised on the assumption of closed deterministic systems, social reality – the reality of many of the practices that are supposed to be developed into evidence-based practices – is anything but a closed deterministic system. Much talk about 'what works', to put it differently, operates on the assumption of a mechanistic ontology that is actually the exception, not the norm in the domain of human interaction, if it occurs at all. This is one of the reasons why 'the extraordinary advances in medicine, agriculture and other fields' that are supposed to have been the result of 'the acceptance by practitioners of evidence as the basis for practice', particularly evidence from the randomized controlled trial (Slavin 2002, p. 16), cannot be expected that easily from a field like education since the dynamics of education are *fundamentally* different from the dynamics of, say, potato growing or chemistry.[8]

I wish to refer to this as the *efficacy deficit* of evidence-based practice, indicating that in the social domain interventions do not generate effects in a mechanistic or deterministic way but through processes that – structurally, not pragmatically – are *open* so that the connections between 'intervention' and 'effect', if those words even make sense, are non-linear and, at most, probabilistic.

---

[8]   This argument can be read as an ontological or as methodological one. Systems theory tends to take the methodological route, arguing that phenomena operate *as if* they were closed, or open, or recursive systems. In terms of notions of causality and how this plays out in social interaction, it can be helpful to make distinctions at the ontological level such as between a causal ontology and a social ontology.

Given the efficacy deficit, one may wonder how anything at all is achieved in the domain of professional action and in the social domain more generally. The answer to this question, as I have made clear in Chapter 2, is called *complexity reduction*. Complexity reduction concerns the reduction of the number of available options for action for the 'elements' of a system. Fast-food restaurants are a good example of a system with reduced complexity as the number of available options for action – both for customers and for staff – is significantly reduced so as to make a quick and smooth operation possible (which also explains why it is so easy to order a hamburger in such fast-food restaurants almost anywhere in the world). The protocols used by call centre workers are another example of complexity reduction, although in those cases the gain is often not in the speed of the process but in its comprehensiveness, that is, making sure that all aspects are covered in an order that is convenient for the call centre worker, not necessarily for the customer. The school, as I have argued, is another prominent example of a system operating under conditions of complexity reduction.

Through complexity reduction, complex open systems generally come to resemble less open systems, that is, systems where there are fewer possible connections between inputs and outputs, between actions and consequences and where, as a result, regularity and structure begin to emerge.[9] Seeing how this is brought about begins to make visible the kind of work – and also the amount of work – that needs to be done in order to create the kind of order in which things can begin to 'work' and in which connections between actions and consequences begin to become more predictable and more secure. Rather than to think of such regularities as naturally occurring phenomena, they are actually in the most literal sense social constructions. To say that these are social constructions is neither to say that they are good nor to say that they are bad. While in some cases complexity reduction can be beneficial, in other cases it can be restraining. But since any attempt to reduce the number of available options for action for the 'elements' within a system is about the exertion of power, complexity reduction should first and foremost be understood as a political act.

---

[9]   A question I will not be able to deal with in this chapter is to what extent attempts to reduce complexity at the very same time increase complexity. For an interesting reflection on this issue, see Rasmussen (2010).

Practice: Application or incorporation?

The idea of complexity reduction is not only important in order to understand why and how it is possible to make things 'work' in complex open systems such as education. It also helps to challenge a claim that is often used to argue that fields such as education should become evidence based. The claim, as quoted above, is that the 'extraordinary advances in medicine, agriculture and other fields' are the *result* of 'the acceptance by practitioners of evidence as the basis for practice', particularly evidence from the randomized controlled trial (Slavin 2002, p. 16). The question this raises is whether it is indeed the case that we should understand the advances in such fields as the result of the application or adoption of scientific knowledge.

One of the most interesting arguments against this way of thinking about the technological success of modern science has been developed by Bruno Latour, particularly in his books *The Pasteurization of France* (Latour 1988) and *Science in Action* (Latour 1987). In these books Latour provides a critique of the epistemological understanding of the influence of modern 'techno-science' (Latour's phrase) on modern society. In the epistemological interpretation the idea is that 'techno-scientists' construct 'facts and machines' in their laboratories which are then distributed to the world outside of the laboratory. The successful distribution of facts and machines to the wider world is generally taken as an indication of the special quality of the knowledge underlying such facts and machines.

While Latour sees no reason to doubt that techno-scientists are able to create effective facts and machines in their laboratories, and while he also does not wish to doubt that at a certain moment in time such facts and machines show up in other places than where they were originally constructed, he does challenge the claim that we should understand this as the application of facts and machines developed in the laboratory in the world outside of the laboratory. Latour suggests that what instead has happened is the transformation of the outside world into the conditions of the laboratory. He writes:

> No one has ever seen a laboratory fact move outside unless the lab is first brought to bear on an 'outside' situation and that situation is transformed so that it fits laboratory prescriptions. (Latour 1983, p. 166)

In his book on Pasteur, Latour argues that the success of Pasteur's approach was not the result of the application of this particular technique across all farms in the French countryside. Pasteur's technique could only work *because* significant dimensions of French farms were first transformed to get them closer to the laboratory conditions under which the technique was developed. As Latour argues, it is 'only on the conditions that you respect a limited set of laboratory practices [that] you can extend to every French farm a laboratory practice made at Pasteur's lab' (Latour 1983, p. 152). The 'pasteurization of France' (Latour 1988) is but one example of how the modern world has changed as a result of modern science, and again and again Latour argues that this is not the result of brining facts and machines into the world 'outside' but of the transformation of the world outside so that it becomes part of the laboratory conditions under which things can work and be true.

Latour refers to 'this gigantic enterprise to make of the outside a world inside of which facts and machines can survive' as *metrology* (Latour 1987, p. 251). Metrology can be understood as a process of creating 'landing strips' for facts and machines (ibid., p. 253). It is a transformation of *society*, an incorporation of society into the network of techno-science, so that facts and machines can 'travel' without any visible effort. There is therefore, as Latour explains, 'no outside of science but there are long, narrow networks that make possible the circulation of scientific facts' (Latour 1983, p. 167). The field where this process is perhaps most visible is that of medicine as much medical knowledge and technology only tend to work under very specific conditions. In some cases, it can be left to individuals to create these conditions – for example by giving instructions that certain medicines should not be combined with alcohol, or should not be used if one is planning to drive a car. But in other cases, medical knowledge and technology can only be made to work under the more strict and controlled conditions of the hospital. From this angle the hospital is a 'halfway house' between the laboratory and the world which makes it possible for medical knowledge and technology to work. While on the one hand we can think of the omnipresence of hospitals, care homes, general practitioners and so on as a beneficial development, it is important to bear in mind how all this is part of a much wider medico-pharmaceutical 'complex' – a vast network of people, things, money, careers, interests that, through its sheer size and number of connections, have made it quite difficult if not impossible to think differently about health and medication and, more importantly, to *do* things differently in this field.

In line with the other two deficits already mentioned, I suggest referring to this aspect as the *application deficit* of evidence-based practice. By this I mean to highlight that to think of the impact of modern science on society in terms of the application of scientific knowledge – which is central to the notion of evidence-based and evidence-informed practice – at least misses important aspects of what makes the application of such knowledge possible (particularly the work that is needed to transform the outside world *so that* knowledge becomes applicable) and perhaps even serves as an ideology that makes the incorporation of practices into particular networks invisible. All this is particularly important because these developments tend to limit the opportunities for people to do and think otherwise – something that can particularly be seen in the ongoing struggles to create opportunities for 'alternative' medicine (and the very phrase 'alternative' already shows the power of what is considered to be 'normal'). It is from here, then, that we can move to questions of normativity, power and values.

From evidence-based to value-based education

I have argued that with regard to the idea of evidence-based practice we can identify three deficits: a *knowledge deficit* (knowledge about the relationships between actions and consequences can only ever provide us with possibilities, never with certainties), an *efficacy deficit* (in most if not all cases of social interaction we have processes that operate as open, recursive systems, as a result of which the connection between actions and consequences can never be totally determined) and an *application deficit* (the idea that practices can change through the application of scientific knowledge makes the work that is done to transform practices so that knowledge can begin to work invisible). These three deficits already raise serious doubts about the 'project' of evidence-based practice and the way in which it is usually presented. In addition, I have introduced the notion of *complexity reduction* as a way to understand how in open recursive semiotic systems it is possible to make things 'work', that is, to create more 'patterned' connections between actions and consequences. The way to do this is to reduce the number of available options for action within the system. I have highlighted that this raises questions about *power*. The issue, after all, is who has the power to reduce options for action for whom. It also raises issues about *normativity* as any deliberate attempt to reduce complexity articulates particular preferences about what is desirable. All this plays a central role in educational practices because education is not simply about any learning or about any influence of teachers on students. Education is a teleological practice – a practice framed by a *telos*, an aim or purpose – which implies that decisions about educational actions and arrangements always have to be taken with an eye on the desirability of what such actions and arrangements are supposed to bring about (see also Biesta 2010f).

The teleological character of education provides us with one important reason for suggesting that questions about 'what works' – that is, questions about the effectiveness of educational actions – are always secondary to questions of purpose. It is only when we have provided an answer to what we hope to achieve that we can begin to ask questions about the ways in which we might be able to achieve such outcomes – bearing in mind all the limitations discussed above. Given that evidence can at most provide us with information about *possible* connections between actions and consequences and therefore is entirely located at the level of the means of education, the idea of evidence-based practice is problematic, because if evidence were the only base for educational practice, educational practice would be entirely without direction. This is one reason why, in education, values come first (see also Ax & Ponte 2010).

This situation is not different in those cases in which proponents of evidence-based practice would go for the less strong option of evidence-*informed* practice. The point again is that if we wish to use any knowledge about possible relationships between actions and consequences, there is still an important judgement to be made as to whether we wish to apply this knowledge and this, again, is a value judgement (see Smith 2006; Biesta 2009b). Such value judgements have two dimensions. On the one hand there is the question of the *general* desirability of information about what might work. The point here is that even if we were able to identify the most effective way of achieving a particular end, we may still want to decide not to act accordingly. There is, for example, important research evidence on the influence of the home environment on educational achievement. Yet in most cases we would find it undesirable to take children away from their parents simply to improve their chances of educational success somewhere down the line. (There are, of course, cases where we do decide that this is the most desirable thing to do, but this is not dictated by knowledge about what works but by complex value judgements about what the most desirable way of action is – which, in this particular example, requires a careful evaluation of potential benefits and potential harm of intervention versus non-intervention.)

In the case of education there is a requirement not only for a general value judgement about the desirability of particular ways of acting but also for what we might refer to as an *educational* value judgement about the means that we can use in education to try to achieve certain desirable outcomes. The reason for this lies in the fact that in education there is an internal relationship between means and ends. The means we use in education – our teaching styles, the ways in which we try to promote certain ways of doing and being – are not neutral with regard to the ends but potentially also teach something to students. Punishment is a good example of this as we may well have strong evidence about the effectiveness of some forms of punishment, and we may even have come to the value judgement that with regard to the use of punishment in a particular situation the benefits outweigh the disadvantages. Yet still we may decide not to use punishment as it would teach children 'that it is appropriate or permissible in the last resort to enforce one's will or get one's own way by the exercise of violence' (Carr 1992, p. 249) – a problem that works out similarly in those cases where the question is whether we should use rewards in education or not.

These points show that values are not simply an element of educational practices but that they are actually *constitutive* of such practices. We might even say that without normative orientations, without decisions about what is educationally desirable, without an articulation of the *telos* of educational practices, these practices simply do not exist – or at least they do not exist as *educational* practices. It is, therefore, only in light of decisions about the aims and ends of educational practices that questions about evidence and effectiveness begin to have any meaning at all. There is, after all, no evidence to generate or collect if we do not first decide about what the aim or purpose of the practice is. This is not to suggest that once such a decision has been made evidence can take over, because to the extent to which evidence can be generated it always needs to be 'filtered' through decisions about what is educationally desirable.

Yet the argument is not simply one between the primacy of values versus the primacy of facts. I have also tried to argue in this chapter that many of the claims about evidence and its capacity to be a basis or source of information for practice are flawed or at least problematic. This is not only because there are limits to the kind of knowledge that can be generated and limits to the extent to which there can be strong and secure links between actions and consequences in the human and social domain. Perhaps the most serious problem for evidence-based practice is that there is actually very little evidence to support the idea that the transformation of such fields as medicine and agriculture is indeed the result of the application of scientific evidence about 'what works' in these fields. The 'project' of evidence-based practice therefore urgently needs to be rethought in ways that take into consideration the limits of knowledge, the nature of social interaction, the ways in which things can work, the processes of power that are involved in this and, most importantly, the values and normative orientations that constitute social practices such as education.

Five questions for discussion and further consideration

1. How might you ensure that findings and insights from your research are not just taken up as evidence about 'what works'?
2. What kind of ideas about knowledge inform your research and where do they sit on the distinction between representation and transaction?
3. Are you able to identify the ways in which the educational situations you are investigating have come about through reduction of complexity (openness, semiosis, recursivity)?
4. To what extent do you consider this reduction of complexity warranted and beneficial? Why?
5. Are there particular conditions that must be in place so that the insights from your research can be relevant for educational practice?

The Practice of Education

So far, I have referred in a rather loose and everyday way to education as a practice. But what does it actually mean to think of education as a practice? What does it include? And also what does it exclude? A good understanding of what a practice is, what would make education into a practice and what the roles of knowledge, understanding and judgement are in educational practices is crucial for educational research – both because the practice of education is often the object of such research and because research, if it seeks to contribute to the improvement of education, needs to feed back into the practice of education. In the late 1960s and early 1970s the American curriculum scholar Joseph Schwab published a number of papers in which he made a case for 'the practical' in education – a case for attention to education as a practice and for a practical rather than 'theoretic' engagement with education. Schwab's ideas were articulated in the context of curriculum research but have relevance for the wider field of educational research. Although in some respects contemporary educational research is quite different from what it was in Schwab's time, there is still much of value in his analysis of and case for 'the practical'. In this chapter I explore his ideas.

Introduction: A case for the practical

In 1969 Joseph Schwab published the first of a series of four papers that argued for a turn to the idea of the 'practical' in curriculum research and practice. In this chapter I revisit the first of these papers in order to explore the extent to which his case for the practical is still relevant today. For this I look at the *past* of the deliberative tradition in which Schwab's arguments are located. Here I suggest that a more explicit engagement with the work of Aristotle – particularly his distinction within the domain of the practical between making and doing and his distinction between knowledge of the eternal and knowledge of the variable – can strengthen Schwab's case, and allows for a better understanding of the kind of knowledge and judgement that is needed in education. In relation to the *present* condition of curriculum research and practice, I highlight three ways in which the current context has changed from when Schwab originally published his paper. These have to do with the strongly diminished space for teachers' professional judgement; the rise of a call for evidence-based education and the transformation of curriculum studies away from the practical questions of everyday education. For the task of reconnecting curriculum studies and educational research more generally with the everyday practice of education, the deliberative approach outlined by Schwab still has much to offer, particularly in light of recent transformations in the research-policy-practice interface. Schwab's ideas are therefore definitely still relevant for the *future* of educational research and practice.

Reading Joseph Schwab's 'The Practical: A Language for Curriculum' (Schwab 1969)[1] about fifty years after it was originally published provides an interesting window on the *longue durée* of curriculum scholarship and on wider trends in educational research, policy and practice. In some respects, Schwab's paper feels remarkably topical, particularly in its ambition to outline a deliberative alternative to the 'technicist' conception of curriculum and curriculum development that still troubles educational practice today, albeit to a certain extent in a different way from when Schwab published his paper. His critique of the curriculum field, and particularly its 'unexamined reliance on theory' (Schwab 2004, p. 103), may also still be relevant today, although, again, there is a significant difference in the kinds of theory that nowadays appear to dominate the field. While his particular analysis of the crisis of the field of curriculum may be less relevant in the current context, the largely Kuhnian approach he takes to the notion of a disciplinary crisis still provides a set of interesting questions for looking at the state of curriculum scholarship and research today, questions that are also relevant for educational research more widely. What is also refreshing is Schwab's focus on the 'classic' questions of curriculum development and improvement, that is, questions about 'what should be taught in our schools, by what means, to whom, under what circumstances, and with what end in view' (Reid 1999, p. 1).

---

[1] I would encourage readers to have a look at Schwab's original text.

There are also aspects that, in hindsight, look more problematic. I am thinking particularly of Schwab's insistence that there is a need to know in detail *'what is and has been going on in American schools'* (ibid., p. 111; emphasis in original) and his suggestion 'to evince the effects of the training [students] did and did not get' (ibid., p. 113). This call for total knowledge of the workings of 'the curricular machine' (itself a rather unfortunate metaphor within a deliberative approach) and of its 'effects' and 'effectiveness' – including effects long after students have left school – could, from a contemporary perspective and when read in isolation, easily be taken as an argument for the technicist forms of school effectiveness research that Schwab actually wants to provide an alternative to.[2]

There are also aspects of Schwab's original paper that appear to be misguided. This is particularly so with the conception of theory Schwab uses in order to articulate the difference between the 'theoretic' (note: not the theoreti*cal*) and the practical. (As I will suggest below, his case *for* the practical is actually far stronger than his case *against* the theoretical.) There are also issues with his use of law as an example of the practical, where he seems to miss the distinction between the normative and the cognitive. And his case for the practical is itself remarkably undertheorized (see also Van Manen 1977). We have to bear in mind, of course, that Schwab's 1969 paper was the first in a series of four (see Schwab 1969, 1971, 1973, 1983[3]) and that these papers were, in turn, part of a wider body of work (see Westbury & Wilkof 1978). While we should not expect, therefore, that all aspects of Schwab's position are developed in detail in this first paper, it is nonetheless sufficiently representative of Schwab's contribution, which is why I will use it as the main source for my reflections.

The past: The deliberative tradition in education

The key issue at stake in the discussion to which Schwab is contributing – and this is in my view one of the enduring issues in the field of curriculum

---

[2] For a nuanced and sympathetic discussion of Schwab's work in relation to these dangers, see Reid (1999).

[3] A longer version of the first paper was published in 1970 by the National Education Association, Center for the Study of Instruction, and was republished in Westbury & Wilkof 1978, pp. 287–321. In this version Schwab provides a more detailed discussion of the practical, the quasi-practical and the eclectic as 'three modes of operation' that are to be distinguished from 'theoretic pursuits' (p. 288).

scholarship and educational theory and research more widely – concerns the question of what kind of practice education actually is. This question has been posed in terms of the 'nature' of the *practice* of education. Here we find distinctions between education as a causal, deterministic system of inputs and outcomes versus education as an open system of meaning, interpretation and understanding; or between education as an anonymous machine versus education as a human encounter; or between education as a process of production versus education as an event. The question about what kind of practice education is has also been posed in terms of the *practising* of education, which brings us back to the old question whether education should be understood as a science or as an art (see, for example, James 1899, pp. 14–15).

Schwab clearly opts for the latter option by highlighting that the practical 'is the discipline concerned with choice and action' and by characterizing 'the very nature of the practical' as being concerned 'with the maintenance and improvement of patterns of purposed action' (Schwab 2004, p. 112). That is why, unlike in the domain of the theoretic where the focus is on the generation of 'warranted conclusions', the orientation in the domain of the practical is on 'defensible decisions' (ibid.). The knowledge needed to navigate in the domain of the practical is therefore characterized by Schwab as 'accumulated lore' with respect to the 'experience of actions and their consequences' (ibid., p. 111). This, in turn, leads him to the point that the method of the practical is *deliberative* rather than deductive or inductive, as it is concerned with 'a decision about action in a concrete situation' (ibid., p. 115). The most crucial aspect of deliberation in the domain of curriculum is that it 'treats both ends and means and must treat them as mutually determining one another' (ibid., p. 116). Deliberation is therefore not just *technical* – it is not just about the means of education – but also *purposeful* in that it is also concerned with the aims and ends of educational action, that is, with 'desiderata in the case' (ibid.). For Schwab this also means that the aim of deliberation is not to choose the *right* alternative – he maintains that 'there is no such thing' in the domain of the practical – 'but the best one' (ibid.).

In addition to this, Schwab argues – in a line of thought not dissimilar to Dewey's case for democracy in *Democracy and Education* (see Dewey 1966) – that because deliberation requires 'consideration of the widest possible variety of alternatives if it is to be most effective' and for each alternative to be viewed 'in the widest variety of lights' (Schwab 2004, p. 116), deliberation also requires 'the formation of a new public and new means of communication amongst its constituent members' (ibid.). For this Schwab believes that a number of barriers need to be removed, including the barriers between education specialists (he mentions the educational psychologist, the philosopher, the sociologist and the test constructor); the barriers between such specialists and teachers, supervisors and school administrators; and the barriers (and hierarchies) between different curriculum subjects, all with the intention to improve communication between all parties (see ibid).

Given the way in which Schwab articulates his case for the practical, it is remarkable that he does not explicitly refer to Aristotle, clearly one of the founding fathers if not *the* founding father of the deliberative tradition in which Schwab situates his case (see Dunne 1992; Reid 1999). This is not to suggest that Schwab's position was not informed by Aristotle's ideas. It clearly was, and traces can not only be found in Schwab's papers but are also evident in his intellectual biography (on the latter, see also the chapter on Schwab in Levine 2006). Yet a more explicit engagement with Aristotle's arguments could have helped Schwab to make a clearer distinction between two aspects that are at stake in the domain of the practical, namely the dimension of *making* (to which Aristotle refers as *poiesis*) and the dimension of *action* (to which he refers as *praxis*), which, in turn, could have helped him to highlight in a more precise manner the different types of knowledge and judgements at stake in the domain of the practical. This could also have helped him to make a more precise case *against* the theoretic, a case in which the target is not scientific knowledge per se, but a particular kind of scientific knowledge, namely knowledge of the eternal as distinct from knowledge of the variable. Let me briefly expand on these two points.

The knowledge we need with regard to *poiesis* is what Aristotle calls *techne* (τέχνη), often translated as art (see Aristotle 1980, p. 141). *Techne*, understood as 'knowledge of how to make things' (ibid., p. 141), is about those activities that have 'an end other than itself' (ibid., p. 143). This means that *techne* is about finding the means that will bring about what one aims to make or bring about. Or in Schwab's terms, *techne* is knowledge about 'actions and their consequences' (ibid., p. 111). *Techne* encompasses knowledge about the materials we work with and about the techniques we can apply to work with those materials. This is never a matter of just following recipes. If, for example, we aim to make a saddle, we need to make judgements about the application of our general knowledge to *this* piece of leather, for *this* horse and for *this* person riding the horse. This is also the case in education, where our judgements are always related to particular students, at particular points in time and in particular situations.

Whereas *poiesis* is about 'how something may come into being which is capable of either being or not being, and whose origin is in the maker and not in the thing made' (Aristotle 1980. p. 141), *praxis* is precisely not about the production of things but about what we might call the promotion of the human good, that is, the promotion of what is conducive 'to the good life in general', as Aristotle puts it (ibid., p. 142). Here the judgement is not about *how* something can be done – the question of *techne* – but about 'what is to be done' (ibid.) – a form of judgement to which Aristotle refers as *phronesis* (φρόνησις), often translated as practical wisdom.[4]

Techne and *phronesis* both require judgement and, in this regard, they clearly are in the domain of 'defensible decisions', not 'warranted conclusions' (Schwab). To a large extent *techne* and *phronesis* coincide with the difference between deliberation about the *means* of education and deliberation about the *ends* of education. While in this regard Aristotle's distinction is helpful in that it highlights the different kinds of judgement at stake – and in this way Aristotle could have provided a theoretical justification for Schwab's turn to the practical – Schwab is right in highlighting that with regard to educational matters deliberation about means can never be separated from deliberation about ends. This is because in education the means we deploy are never neutral with regard to the ends, since students pick up as much (and even more) from what we *do* as from what we *say*. (Many students are also very good at spotting any contradictions between the two.)

The second way in which Aristotle could have helped Schwab's argument has to do with the distinction Aristotle makes between the domain of the *eternal* – the domain of necessity, that is, of things 'ungenerated and imperishable' (Aristotle 1980, p. 140) – and the domain of the *variable* – the domain where *poiesis* and *praxis* are located (ibid., p. 141). The distinction is

---

[4] It is instructive to see that the word 'wisdom' figures prominently in Schwab's paper, particularly in his discussion of the practical, the quasi-practical and the eclectic, although he never clearly articulates the – importance of the – difference between *poiesis* and *praxis*.

important not only because it provides a useful vocabulary for the description of the reality of education as having to do with variable matters – with actions and consequences – rather than with the eternal and unchangeable, but also because of the difference it makes between knowledge of the eternal – which Aristotle calls *episteme* (ἐπιστήμη), often translated as scientific knowledge (see ibid., p. 140) – and knowledge and judgement in the domain of the variable (*techne* and *phronesis*). The main benefit of Aristotle's distinction is that it highlights that most of what Schwab says about theory and most of the problems he has with the use of theory in the curriculum field actually refers to theory as *episteme* – knowledge of the eternal – and not of theory as *techne* and *phronesis*. Using Aristotle in this way would, on the one hand, have allowed Schwab to be far less 'anti theory' as he appears to be in his paper and would, on the other hand, have allowed him to make a much more positive case for the kinds of theory we need in the domain of the variable (see also Biesta, Allan & Edwards 2011; Van Manen 1977).

That Schwab's critique of theory in the field of curriculum is mainly informed by a notion of knowledge as *episteme* – knowledge of the eternal – can also be seen in his discussion of theory and representation where he argues that because theories are always selective – they look from a particular angle, a particular set of assumptions – they are necessarily incomplete as representations ('pale and incomplete representation of actual behaviour' – ibid., p. 111). If knowledge is indeed understood as the representation of a reality 'out there' then the distinction between knowledge of the eternal and knowledge of the variable makes sense, and then Schwab may have a point in arguing that knowledge about the eternal is never sufficient in the domain of action and hence 'knowledge of some other kind derived from another source' is needed (ibid., p. 111).

The fact that Schwab conceives of theory first and foremost in terms of representation also causes some problems when he brings in law as an example of the kind of knowledge/theory that is appropriate for the domain of the practical. The point here is not, as Schwab argues, that 'servants of the law must know the law through and through' (ibid., p. 112), but rather has to do with a crucial distinction between the domain of the cognitive and the domain of the normative. The laws that 'servants of the law' need to have knowledge about are, after all, not descriptions or representations of legal reality but are *prescriptions* in that they provide guidance for legal judgement. They are, therefore, not cognitive but *normative*. Schwab's reference to law thus reveals that in human practices such as education there is never just the technical question of how to do things but always also the normative question of what to do, that is, of what to aim for, as I have already discussed in more detail in the previous chapters.

The present: What is different?

With regard to the main point made by Schwab that curriculum needs to be approached in terms of the practical, not the theoretic, I am therefore inclined to agree. I think that Schwab's intuitions about the nature of the educational endeavour are basically correct, although his presentation is on the unhelpful side, not least because of his use of a too strong opposition between the theoretic and the practical. What he says about the practical is, again, basically sound, although a more explicit reference to Aristotle could have helped to highlight with more precision the different kinds of judgement and knowledge at stake in the domain of the practical and to distinguish more explicitly between the making and the acting dimensions of education. Where things become problematic is in the conception of theoretical knowledge Schwab uses to construct his argument, because he mainly seems to refer to *episteme* which, following Aristotle, is the kind of knowledge that actually has nothing to do in the domain of the variable. I am inclined to conclude, therefore, that the case for the practical still stands and that, over the years, it has actually gained in strength as a result of the contributions of other scholars who take inspiration from Aristotle and the deliberative tradition more widely (see, for example, Kessels & Korthagen 1996; Reid 1999; Coulter & Wiens 2002). But one of the key questions is *in what context* this case still stands, and here things have changed significantly since Schwab's original publication. I wish to identify three important changes.

One of the crucial implications that follow from Schwab's suggestions for a practical 'turn' has to do with the central role of teacher judgement. After all, in practical domains such as education we are always involved in 'a decision about action in a concrete situation' (ibid., p. 115), that is, in deliberation and judgement about the concrete means and the concrete ends of our actions. Schwab correctly points out that such deliberation is first of all concrete and situated and that, in that sense, it is fundamentally 'of the teacher'. However, he also highlights the need for deliberation across a wider constituency – the public dimension of deliberation – so that judgement can be shared, tested and collectively supported. It is first and foremost with regard to teacher judgement that things have changed significantly over the past two decades as a result of the unprecedented interference of politicians and policy makers with the minutiae of education in many countries around the world (see, for example, Gewirtz 2001). This has often happened in relation to the rise of neoliberal regimes of accountability that more often than not tend to distort rather than support educational practices and processes.

The rise of top-down prescription of both the content and the form of education – the 'what' and the 'how' – has significantly diminished the opportunities for teachers to exert judgement, individually and collectively, and has rather put them under a regime of the constant measurement of educational 'outcomes'. The further intervention of supranational organizations such as the OECD and the World Bank has put additional pressure on the space for professional action and judgement, where we also shouldn't forget that this development is not unique for education but has happened in many other professional fields (see, for example, Noordegraaf & Abma 2003; Noordegraaf 2007). The crucial question this raises is not only how a case for the practical can still be made in the current political context but also how such a case can make an impact in a significantly different political context for contemporary education. The latter point is the more important one, as there is not so much a shortage of critiques of current education policy trends but much more a shortage of viable alternatives.[5]

Secondly, Schwab was arguing against a particular form of research that appeared to dominate curriculum and educational scholarship at the time. His arguments seem to be targeted at what is often referred to as positivistic research, although it is perhaps better to characterize it as scientistic, that is, based on a particular belief in the power of 'science', narrowly conceived. However, since the publication of Schwab's paper, the field of educational

---

[5] This is not to suggest that such alternatives are entirely absent or that education policy around the world operates in one and the same (depressing) mode. For an analysis of different trends in recent curriculum policy and practice, taking Scotland's new Curriculum for Excellence as a 'case', see Priestley & Biesta (2013). And for an insight in the dynamics of teacher agency – its conditions, limitations and possibilities – see Priestley, Biesta & Robinson (2015).

and curriculum research has also changed significantly. There are two, partly opposite trends. Particularly in the English-speaking world there is now a plethora of what is often referred to as qualitative research (although I think it is more accurate to call it interpretative research; see Biesta 2010b), which, rather than making grand claims about what 'is', explores in much detail dimensions of educational experience and interpretation, often in the form of small-scale studies of concrete practices. While in a sense this can be seen as the kind of knowledge about *'what is and has been going on in American schools'* (ibid., p. 111; emphasis in original) that Schwab was calling for, it is important to acknowledge that Schwab was much more after more practical forms of knowledge – knowledge about relationships between educational actions and consequences – and less after descriptions and interpretations of educational experiences and practices. It is here that some of what Schwab was suggesting appears to be more in line with a second major change in the field of educational research, which concerns the rise of investigations into educational effectiveness and a call for the conduct of scientific research into 'what works' so as to generate an evidence base for educational practice – a development discussed in the two previous chapters.

These two trends – the explosion of small-scale interpretative and ethnographic studies of education on the one hand and the strong push for research on effectiveness and 'what works' on the other – provide a significantly different environment than what was the case when Schwab presented his ideas. While at a superficial level it may look as if what Schwab was advocating has become reality in the second line of development – effectiveness and 'what works' – a more nuanced reading of Schwab's position suggests that he was actually after a third option that would take questions about effectiveness seriously, but as practical and situated questions that require deliberation about means and ends rather than as questions that can be addressed and solved at the level of research and then be turned into prescriptions for educational practice.[6]

A third way in which the current situation is significantly different from the time when Schwab wrote his paper has to do with the development of the field of curriculum scholarship itself. Looking at the field from a Continental

---

[6]   This is also how Reid (1999) reads Schwab, and I am inclined to agree with his reading.

position I can discern two trends. One, particularly prevalent in North America but with a global impact on the field, is the reconceptualization of curriculum studies away from issues of curriculum development and improvement in the context of schooling towards the wider understanding of curriculum in its biographical, sociocultural, historical and political dimensions (see Pinar 1975; Pinar et al. 1995; Pinar 1999). This development has definitely deepened understandings of the complexities of curriculum as it 'occurs' in schools and other settings, but has, in some cases, turned the curriculum field into a form of cultural studies that, according to some, has lost connection with its 'core business' (see, for example. Westbury 2007) – albeit that one of the questions at stake in the reconceptualization of curriculum and curriculum studies was precisely about what the 'core business' of the field is and who should have the right to define this.

While particularly in some of his other publications Schwab developed his case for the practical in very concrete concerns about how curriculum development in schools ought to be organized and how university-based professors and university-educated curriculum specialists should contribute to this task (see also Schwab 1983), Schwab's more general case for the practical clearly keeps the focus more strongly on the 'doing' rather than just on the 'understanding' of curriculum, and in this sense provides an approach that is different from the cultural 'turn' that curriculum scholarship has taken in North America. Yet Schwab's approach also appears to be different from the way in which the field of curriculum has perhaps developed more strongly on the Continent, that is, as the empirical study of the technicalities of learning and instruction. Here curriculum scholarship seems to have turned into the study of 'teaching-and-learning' and also into the field of what, in some circles, is known as the 'learning sciences'. If the reconceptualization of curriculum studies perhaps moved the field much closer to 'why' questions – and thus to the domain of *praxis* – the turn towards the empirical study of learning and instruction has moved the field predominantly to 'how' questions – and thus to the domain of *poiesis*, albeit often more with technological ambitions than in terms of Aristotelian *techne*.

Schwab – or more accurately, an updated version of Schwab's deliberative approach – may still provide a framework for a middle position between the two. Such a position is, on the one hand, more concerned with the practicalities of curriculum development and improvement than where the turn towards understanding curriculum has taken the field, yet is, on the other hand, better aware of the intrinsic relationship between the means and ends of education and the significance of the question of purpose than where the turn towards the learning sciences has taken the field. If in the first case there is perhaps now too much theory in the field of curriculum, in the second case there is definitely too little – a situation which may give new meaning to Schwab's claim about the field's 'unexamined reliance on theory'.

The future: Where to go and what to do?

In my discussion of Schwab's paper and the wider deliberative tradition of which his work is a part, I have suggested that the turn towards the practical provides a middle position between a number of extremes. Schwab's turn to the practical is clearly focused on the practicalities of curriculum development and improvement and in this sense stays closer to the everyday practice of education than those developments in curriculum scholarship that have focused much more on understanding rather than 'doing' curriculum. Yet this does *not* lead Schwab to an approach that is just interested in the technicalities of instruction without any concern for the normative questions that inevitably are at stake in any educational endeavour. One could say, in other words, that the deliberative approach that is at the heart of Schwab's 'practical turn' provides us with an important educational reminder vis-à-vis current developments in the curriculum field – and perhaps we can even call it an educational 'corrective'.

My reason for calling it an *educational* corrective has to do with the fact that Schwab's case for the practical is able to capture a number of key dimensions of educational processes and practices. These include (1) the experimental nature of education, that is, the fact that educational action is fundamentally open towards the future and always operates with the relationship between actions and *possible* consequences rather than on the 'logic' of intervention and predictable effect; (2) the purposeful nature of education, that is, the fact that education, unlike learning or 'just being together', always aims for something (leaving open the question who sets the aims or ought to set the aims) and (3) the fact that education is never (only) a matter of the production of certain things (such as learning outcomes) but always also aims to contribute to the promotion of the human good, or, in Aristotle's terms, 'the good life in general' (again leaving open the question what the human good is and who is or ought to be involved in articulating conceptions of the human good). In all this, Schwab's approach acknowledges the 'reality' of education in a way that the turn towards education as effective intervention does not.

What I also find attractive about Schwab's particular articulation of the practical is his attention for the *public* dimensions of deliberation. Here he clearly takes questions about the shape, form and direction of curricular processes and practices away from individual taste and preference, towards the level of *public* and hence potentially *democratic* deliberation. In Schwab's hands the turn towards the practical in curriculum scholarship does therefore not endorse a romantic notion of context-less interactions between teachers and learners but lifts it explicitly to the level of the collective, the democratic and the political. While the reconceptualization of curriculum studies has contributed much to deepening our understanding of curriculum as a 'political text' (Pinar et al. 1995), Schwab's insistence on the need for public forms of curricular deliberation turns political understanding into political action – or at least has the potential for doing so. This is particularly important given the changing nature of the political context of contemporary schooling in many countries around the world, a political context that not only encompasses the politics of schooling but also includes the politics of educational research, as I have already discussed in previous chapters and will return to later in this book.

Conclusion

What, in conclusion, might this imply for the future of curriculum scholarship and research? Perhaps the most concise way of putting it, is that Schwab's case for a practical turn urges us to (re)connect with the *doing* of curriculum rather than only or exclusively with understanding it (which is, of course, not meant to create a new opposition between doing and understanding but to point at the dangers of understanding without engagement with the doing). The doing of curriculum needs to be read with a double emphasis. On the one hand it suggests, as mentioned, the importance of engagement with the *doing* of curriculum; on the other hand it suggests the importance of engagement with the doing of *curriculum*, so as not to dissolve key educational questions about content, purpose and relationships into formal questions about processes and techniques, particularly if such work is completely disconnected from engagement with the question of educational purpose. Such scholarship needs to be explicitly political, not so much in its mode of analysis as in its mode of operation – that is, that it needs to be conducted as a form of public scholarship, scholarship that promotes public deliberation about the means and, most importantly, the ends of education. While Schwab's original paper is perhaps not the most sophisticated and successful articulation of a deliberative approach to curriculum – which is why I have highlighted above where and how his approach needs updating – it nonetheless stands as an important reminder of a mode of curricular scholarship that is distinctively educational, both in its theoretical substance and in its practical orientation.

Five questions for discussion and further consideration

1. It is easy to refer to education as a practice. How, with the help of ideas and concepts from this chapter, might you be able to identify the distinctive dimensions of a practice?
2. Looking at your own research, how would you reflect on its ambitions in terms of the distinction between (knowledge of) the eternal and (knowledge of) the variable?
3. And how would you reflect on the ambitions of your research in terms of the distinction between *poiesis* and *praxis*?
4. Where and how does what kind of notion of curriculum play a part in your research?
5. Schwab argues that deliberation in education is not just a matter of individuals, such as teachers, but needs to become public. Do you agree? What would it mean for your own research?

5

Configurations of Educational Research

The ongoing rise of the English language as the 'lingua franca' of research in education and almost all other fields seems to suggest that research is roughly the same everywhere, irrespective of what languages are being used to talk about research and do research. It also seems to suggest that translation between languages is relatively easy and that English is a kind of neutral conduit. The omnipresence of the English language may give us the impression that this is so, but anyone who has command of another language than English may know that translation is not that easy. And anyone who has knowledge of educational practices and traditions of educational research as they have developed in other linguistic contexts and settings may have some awareness that things are not everywhere the same. In this chapter I will focus on two 'configurations' of educational research, comparing the way in which the field of research has developed in the English-speaking world (focusing on England) with the way in which the field of research has developed in the German-speaking world (focusing on Germany). The purpose of this chapter is first of all to show that educational research is not one thing but that there are quite different configurations of research in different contexts and settings. Comparing the Anglo-American configuration with the Continental one also helps to identify strengths and weaknesses of both configurations and thus, for each configuration, in gaining a perspective on its own 'blind spots'.

Introduction

In the English-speaking world educational research is commonly conceived as the inter- or multidisciplinary study of educational processes and practices.

Hence research in education strongly relies on theoretical input from a range of different academic disciplines. Historically the four most prominent ones have been philosophy, history, psychology and sociology, albeit that their respective influence has fluctuated over time (see McCulloch 2002). While some have argued that the influence of this particular configuration has decreased in recent years (see, for example, Bridges 2006), it not only still provides an important frame of reference for discussions about the present and future of educational research (see, for example, Lawn & Furlong 2009; Pollard & Oancea 2010) but also still exerts an important influence on the social organization of the field (see Lawn & Furlong 2007). What is virtually absent in what, in this chapter, I will refer to as the Anglo-American[1] configuration of the field is the idea of education as an academic discipline in its own right. In this regard this configuration differs significantly from the way in which the study of education has developed in Continental Europe, particularly in the German-speaking world.[2] Here the study of education has developed more explicitly as a separate academic discipline with its own forms and traditions of theorizing.

The fact that the academic study of education has developed so differently within different contexts not only raises important historical questions about the events that have brought about these different configurations (see for example Keiner 2002). From a contemporary perspective there is also the question as to what can be learned from a dialogue between the different configurations of the field.[3] Within the confines of this chapter I am particularly interested in the question whether there are forms of theory and theorizing that are distinctively *educational* rather than that they are generated through 'other' disciplines. The reason for approaching this question in terms of disciplinarity is not because I am searching for some kind of 'essence' of the field of education – disciplinary boundaries are, after all, socio-historical

---

[1] Although my discussion in this chapter will be confined to the British – and perhaps it is even more accurate to say English – construction of the field of educational studies, the particular construction of the field I will discuss is also prominent in North America and other English-speaking countries. This is the reason why I refer to this construction as 'Anglo-American' rather than English or British.

[2] The influence of this way of approaching the study of education is not confined to countries where German is the main or one of the main languages, but has also impacted on countries such as the Netherlands, Belgium, Denmark, Norway, Finland and Poland.

[3] I take inspiration from a project conducted by Bjørg Gundem, Stefan Hopmann and colleagues, who aimed to compare the Continental tradition of 'Didaktik' with the American tradition of curriculum studies (see Gundem & Hopmann 1998).

constructions (see Gieryn 1983, 1999; Van Hilvoorde 2002) – but because it is a useful way for characterizing the different configurations of the academic study of education and, more importantly, because it allows to focus more directly on the different ways in which theoretical resources are being deployed in the study of education.

In what follows I provide a comparative reconstruction of what I will refer to as the Anglo-American and the Continental configuration of the field of educational studies.[4] I discuss aspects of the particular histories of these configurations and engage with the reasons that have been given for conceiving and constructing the study of education in these particular ways. This will not only allow me to highlight where and how these two configurations differ, but also make it possible to show what is specific about each of these configurations and how and why these specificities might matter for contemporary discussions about the study of education and the role theory may play in it. The main ambition of this chapter is to show that the study of education *can* be constructed differently and *has* been constructed differently.

The Anglo-American configuration

As McCulloch (2002) has shown in his overview of the development of educational studies in Britain since the 1950s, the idea that the study of education cannot proceed without contributions from (other) disciplines has been the dominant view throughout the second half of the twentieth century even if, as he argues, this period has been characterized by a rise and a subsequent decline of the dominance of the disciplines (see also Lawn and Furlong 2009). In order to understand the history of this particular configuration,

---

[4] The two constructions presented in this chapter should themselves be understood as constructed. They are, in a sense, ideal types meant to make sense of differences between the ways in which the study of education has developed in Britain and Germany (and in both cases these developments have impacted on the organization of the academic study of education in other countries and contexts). As I will argue in the concluding section of this chapter, the two traditions are, to a certain degree, incommensurable in that they operate on the basis of fundamentally different assumptions and ideas. This is neither to suggest that communication between the two is impossible nor to suggest that the two traditions have developed independently from each other. There is ample evidence of interplay, interaction and connection between the two configurations of the field, for example the popularity of Herbartianism in late-nineteenth-century Britain and North America, the appropriation of Piagetian psychology in the United States or the influence of Wundt on pragmatism. From this angle it is perhaps even more remarkable that the study of education has developed in such diverging ways.

the reasons given for it and some of the social and sociological dimensions, I will, in this section, focus on one exemplary case, which is a book published in 1966 under the editorship of J. W. Tibble called *The Study of Education* (Tibble 1966a). McCulloch (2002, p. 106) has called the book 'probably the best-known published work of the period to promote a disciplinary approach to educational studies', which is a key reason for focusing on the 'case' of this book. McCulloch's reconstruction shows that the particular conception of educational studies presented in this book can be found in almost identical form in a number of key publications preceding and following the publication of Tibble's 1966 book.

Tibble's book is first of all interesting because it is indeed a 'paradigm case' of the configuration of the field of educational studies as an inter- or multidisciplinary field based on theoretical input from four 'contributing' (Tibble 1966b, p. vii) or 'fundamental' (Hirst 1966, p. 57) disciplines: philosophy, history, psychology and sociology. The book is also interesting because it provides an explicit rationale for this particular configuration, arguing that the principles of educational theory 'stand or fall entirely on the validity of the knowledge contributed by [the fundamental disciplines]' (Hirst 1996, p. 50). Thirdly, the book is interesting because it was intended as a deliberate intervention in the field of educational studies in the UK in order to give the field more structure and (academic) status (see also McCulloch 2002). *The Study of Education* was the 'central volume' of *The Students Library of Education*, a series consisting of at least seventeen further volumes (as announced on the paper cover of *The Study of Education*) with Tibble as the main editor and with an editorial board consisting of Ben Morris, Richard Peters, Brian Simon and William Taylor who also were the respective authors of the chapters on the psychology, philosophy, history and sociology of education in the book. Tibble's own chapter 'The development of the study of education' (Tibble 1966c) is particularly helpful as it provides his reconstruction of the situation in which the book series was supposed to intervene.

Tibble locates the study of education firmly within the context of 'the professional preparation of teachers' (Tibble 1966c, p. 1). Although the connection with teacher education provides the study of education with an institutional context and a clear raison d'être, he emphasizes that because of the historically peripheral status of teacher education within the university – the main institutional setting for teacher education were non-university-based colleges of education – the development of education 'as a subject of study in its own right' has been limited (Tibble 1966b, p. viii). Tibble notes that 'with a few exceptions (e.g. Wales and Sheffield) it has no place as a subject in undergraduate courses' (Tibble 1966c, p. 1), which also explains why it has not been easy 'to develop close links between the study of education and the basic disciplines which contribute to it' (ibid.). This problem is replicated at the level of higher degree courses, so Tibble argues, 'mainly because of the non-existence of education as a first degree subject, thus denying a basis for higher education' (Tibble 1966c, p. 2).

For universities this has created the situation where they have to accept either 'non-graduates who are well qualified in education' – and Tibble adds that most universities do not admit non-graduates to higher degrees – or 'graduates in other subjects with no study of education beyond the initial training stage' (ibid.). This is also one of the main causes of 'a very serious shortage of adequately qualified lecturers in education' (ibid.). Tibble identifies the expansion of higher education in the UK following the Robbins Report (1963) as the main reason for 'the present ferment of discussion about the study of education' (Tibble 1966c, p. 2) and credits the colleges of education with providing the main impetus for this discussion. It was particularly the development of four-year BEd degrees in education instead of one-year professional training programmes for teachers that provided the context for the attention to the structure and form of, and the rationale for, the study of education. This is not to suggest, of course, that education had not been studied before, and the majority of Tibble's chapter provides an overview 'of the historical development of this study over the 120 years since the training of teachers was inaugurated in this country' (ibid., p. 3).

The picture that emerges from this is one where, until the first decades of the twentieth century, teacher education was mainly practice based – Tibble specifically mentions the so-called 'pupil teacher system developed in Holland' (ibid., p. 3) – which some saw as a good thing and others not. While Andrew Bell early in the nineteenth century would argue that it is 'by attending the school, seeing what is going on there, and taking a share in the office of tuition, that teachers are to be formed, and not by lectures and abstract instructions' (Bell quoted in Tibble 1966c, p. 4), C. H. Judd in his *The Training of Teachers in England, Scotland and Germany* (1914) laments 'the relative neglect of education theory' in teacher education, writing that 'one is tempted to say that the teachers in English training colleges have not realized the possibility of dealing in a scientific way with the practical problems of school organization and the practical problems which come up in the conduct of recitations' (Judd quoted in Tibble 1966c, p. 5). Tibble notes, however, that around the turn of the century some more theoretical strands were beginning to creep into 'the embryonic study of education' (ibid., p. 6). These were the study of method, of the history of education and, increasingly, of educational psychology, a field which became more firmly established as a subject of study in the 1920s (see ibid., p. 10), although a first edition of the *Teacher's Handbook of Psychology* had already appeared in 1886 (see ibid., p. 8).

The Herbartian theory of learning 'with its "scientific" prescription for the organization of the lesson' is listed as 'a dominant influence' during this period (ibid., p. 9), also because of the influence of a book with the title *The Herbartian Psychology Applied to Education*, published in 1897 by John Adams, first principal of the London Day Training College (see ibid., p. 11). Another influential book was Percy Nunn's *Education, its Data and First Principles* (first published in 1920, with a second edition in 1930 and a third in 1945), which heavily relied on William McDougall's 'hormic' psychology (see ibid, pp. 11–12). There was also an emerging interest in child study, partly as a result of the rise of progressive education and further through the work of Jean Piaget, whose writings became available in English in 1926. Psychology remained an important pillar of teacher education during this period (see ibid., pp. 12–19).

The second main strand Tibble identifies in the development of the study of education is that of the history of education, which includes comparative education and the study of great educators (ibid., p. 19). Tibble documents a substantial amount of activity in this field from the late nineteenth century onwards, both in terms of book publications and with regard to the inclusion of history of education in the curriculum of teacher education programmes. He also notes that 'history provides the largest number of intending teachers who have a first degree qualification in the field of study' so that, also compared to the psychology, philosophy and sociology of education, there is 'no lack of historians who are prepared to apply their skills to the study of the history of education' (ibid., pp. 20–21). Nonetheless, 'under the intense pressure of the two year course, and with the main emphasis on educational psychology (...) historical studies were relatively meagre' within the programmes of teacher education colleges (ibid., p. 21).[5] Tibble was also not very optimistic about the future role of history of education in four-year BEd courses because of the fact 'that college students in general prefer educational studies where the short term application from theory to practice is most evident' and many of them 'do not readily "see the point" of historical studies' (ibid.).

For Tibble the sociology and philosophy of education 'barely come within the scope of a historical survey' because their history is 'too recent' (ibid., p. 21). This is not to suggest that no attention has been paid within teacher education curricula and programmes to social and philosophical questions, but Tibble's reconstruction gives the impression that the development of sociology and philosophy of education as separate fields of study has only been of a recent date (a point confirmed by McCulloch 2002). This, together with the very prominent position of the psychology and, to a lesser extent, the history of education, explains the absence of *systematic* attention to the sociology and philosophy of education within the education of teachers, although Tibble does mention the presence of works by philosophers such as Dewey, Whitehead, Russell, Campagnac and Nunn on the book lists of department and college courses (see ibid., p. 24).

Three things stand out in Tibble's account of the development of the study of education in England. One is the fact that the context for the study of education is teacher education. This suggests that the field of education is mainly understood in terms of schooling and school education. Secondly, Tibble provides a number of reasons why the institutional 'reproduction' of the study of education is relatively weak. One reason is the absence of education as an undergraduate subject. This has impacted negatively on the educational focus of higher degree work (such work rather was 'framed' through the contributing disciplines) but also on the availability of academic staff with experience and expertise in the study of education. Thirdly, Tibble's discussion is strongly framed in terms of four contributing disciplines. Of these, psychology seems to have had the strongest hold on the education of teachers,

---

[5]　It is interesting to note that the first Handbook of Research on Teaching in the United States was published in 1965. Since this handbook was edited by an educational psychologist (Nathaniel Gage, from Stanford, who was appointed editor by AERA), this handbook serves as another indication that psychology was the preferred/dominant foundational discipline for the field of education at that time.

with history at a distant second place. At the time when Tibble was writing, philosophy and sociology were only emerging as contributing disciplines for the study of education.

The case for educational theory

While Tibble provides a historical and, to a certain extent, sociological account of the development of the study of education, Paul Hirst's contribution to *The Study of Education* takes a more systematic approach in that he aims to provide a rationale for a particular configuration of the study of education. Hirst does this under the heading of 'educational theory' arguing that such questions as 'What is educational theory, as a theoretical pursuit, trying to achieve? How does this theory relate to educational practice? What kind of theoretical structure has it got and how in fact do the various elements that are obviously a part of it fit in it?' have received 'far too little sustained attention' (Hirst 1966, p. 30). As a result 'educational studies have tended to become either a series of unrelated or even competing theoretical pursuits, or a confused discussion of educational problems where philosophical, psychological, sociological or historical and other issues jostle against one another, none being adequately dealt with' (ibid.) – echoing Richard Peters's characterization of the field in 1963 as an 'undifferentiated mush' (Peters 1963, p. 273). This is why Hirst aims to move towards 'a more adequate framework within which research and teaching in this area can develop' (Hirst 1966, p. 30).

Hirst puts forward a very specific and very precise notion of educational theory. Starting from O'Connor's (1957) distinction between theory as 'a set or system of rules or a collection of precepts which guide or control actions of various kinds' and theory as 'a single hypothesis or a logically interconnected set of hypotheses that have been confirmed by observation' (Hirst 1966, p. 38) he, unlike O'Connor, opts for the former rather than the latter as the most appropriate notion of theory for education. 'Educational theory is in the first place to be understood as the essential background to rational educational practice not as a limited would-be scientific pursuit' (ibid., p. 40). The reason for this has to do with his view about the function of theory in practical activities. Whereas 'in the case of the empirical sciences, a theory is a body of statements that have been subjected to empirical tests and which express our understanding of certain aspects of the physical world' – something which Schwab would refer to as the 'theoretic' – in the case of 'a practical activity like education' theory 'is not the end product of the pursuit, but rather it is constructed to determine and guide the activity' (ibid., p. 40) – close to Schwab's understanding of and argument for 'the practical'. Hirst thus makes a distinction between educational theory in a narrow and a wider sense. The first concerns 'the body of scientific knowledge on which rational educational judgments rest', while the second refers to 'the whole enterprise of building a body of rational principles for educational practice' (ibid., p. 41).

Hirst is not arguing that one of these notions of theory is the correct one but rather emphasizes that we neither should reduce educational theory to the former conception (as O'Connor prefers) nor should conflate the two types of theory. Hirst also believes that it is 'on the development of the theory in its larger sense that educational practice depends, not simply on the development of scientific study' (ibid.), although the latter is an important component of the former. Educational theory in the wider sense is therefore 'not concerned simply with producing explanations on the scientific model *but with forming rationally justified principles for what ought to be done in an area of practical activity*' (ibid., p. 42, emphasis added) – again quite close to Schwab's case for 'the practical'. This, according to Hirst, is why the difference between 'scientific theory' and 'educational theory' is not a difference of degree or scale but expresses a *logical* difference between judgements about 'what is the case' and 'what ought to be the case' (ibid.) – or, to be more precise, about 'what ought to be done in educational activities' (ibid., p. 53). Hirst concludes therefore that there is 'a great deal to be said for characterizing these theories under moral knowledge' because he sees it as a fundamental task of theory to make 'value judgements about what exactly is to be aimed at in education' (ibid., p. 52), not in a general sense but at a practical level and in 'here-and-now' terms.

Hirst thus articulates a conception of educational theory as a form of practical theory, the purpose of which is *not* the generation of scientific truth but the development of 'rationally justified principles' for educational action. In this guise educational theory *mediates* between the contributions of '[philosophy], history, social theory, psychological theory and so on' (ibid., p. 33) on the one hand and educational practice on the other. This view has several important implications. One is that educational theory is not simply derivative of factual knowledge because factual knowledge in itself can never provide a sufficient justification for what ought to be done. In this sense we might say that the resources for educational theory are 'composite' in that they consist of reasons for educational principles that are 'of an empirical, philosophical, moral or other logical kind' (ibid., p. 51). This also means that educational theory is *not* 'in the last analysis philosophical in character' (ibid., p. 30), because philosophy in itself cannot provide all that is needed to generate and justify principles for educational action. It can only provide one sort of reasons to inform such principles.

The most interesting point for the discussion, however, follows from Hirst's claim that the validity of the principles for educational action 'turns on nothing "educational" beyond these [reasons]' (ibid., p. 51). He argues that the reasons that inform educational principles must be judged solely according to the standards of the particular disciplines they stem from. 'The psychological reasons must be shown to stand to the strict canons of that science. Equally the historical, philosophical or other truths that are appealed to must be judged according to the criteria of the relevant discipline in each case' (ibid.). This lies at the very heart of Hirst's claim that educational theory is not and cannot be 'an autonomous discipline' (ibid., p. 51) because it does not generate 'some unique form of understanding about education' in addition to what is generated through the 'fundamental' disciplines (for this term, see ibid., p. 57). The principles of educational theory 'stand or fall entirely on the validity of the knowledge contributed by [the fundamental disciplines]' (ibid., 50). Hirst summarizes his views by arguing, on the one hand, that educational theory 'is not itself an autonomous "form" of knowledge or an autonomous discipline. It involves no conceptual structure unique in its logical features and no unique tests for validity', while on the other hand, educational principles 'are justified entirely by direct appeal to knowledge from a variety of forms, scientific, philosophical, historical, etc. Beyond these forms of knowledge, it requires no theoretical synthesis' (ibid., p. 55).

Hirst's conception of educational theory provides a strong rationale for the Anglo-American configuration of the field of educational studies, not only because it denies any autonomous disciplinary status to educational theory but also – and for this very reason – because it locates all the 'rigorous work' within the fundamental disciplines 'according to their own critical canons' (ibid., p. 55). It thus necessarily makes the study of education into the *inter- or multidisciplinary* study of the 'phenomenon' of education to which educational theory itself has no cognitive contribution to make. This, in turn, is the reason for it lacking a disciplinary status *among* other disciplines. Tibble, in a book from 1971 called *An Introduction to the Study of Education* (Tibble 1971a), summarizes this point of view in the following way:

> It is clear that 'education' is a field subject, not a basic discipline; there is no distinctively 'educational' way of thinking; in studying education one is using psychological or historical or sociological or philosophical ways of thinking to throw light on some problem in the field of human learning. (Tibble 1971b, p. 16)

When from here we turn our attention to the development of the field in Continental Europe, a rather different picture emerges.

The Continental configuration

The first thing to mention with regard to the Continental configuration of the field of educational studies is that of language – and to assume that within the Continental configuration there is such a thing as 'the field of educational studies' is in a sense already a misrepresentation. Whereas in the English language the word 'education' suggests a certain conceptual unity, the German language has (at least) two different words to refer to the *object* of study – 'Erziehung' and 'Bildung' – and a number of different words that refer to the study of 'Erziehung' and 'Bildung', such as 'Pädagogik', 'Didaktik', 'Erziehungswissenschaft' or 'Erziehungswissenschaften' (plural), 'Bildungs-wissenschaft' and 'Bildungswissenschaften' (plural). Although 'Erziehung' and 'Bildung' are not entirely separate concepts, they do represent different aspects of and approaches to educational processes and practices. For reasons of space I will, in what follows, focus on 'Erziehung' and 'Pädagogik'.

The concept of 'Erziehung' is of a younger date than that of 'Bildung'. Oelkers (2001, p. 30) explains that 'Erziehung' only became used as a noun in the German language from the Reformation onwards. With Luther, 'Erziehung' came to refer to influences that in some way impact on the soul of the human being in order to bring about a virtuous personality, initially understood in terms of Christian virtues but later expanded so as to include secular virtues as well (see ibid., p. 31). Although this is a central idea in the conceptual history of the notion of 'Erziehung', Oelkers emphasizes that the word 'Erziehung' does not refer to one single reality. 'Erziehung' can, for example, be used in relation to processes, institutions, situations or aims (ibid., p. 24), and can be characterized as dialogue or action, as communication, influence or development, as process or product, as restriction or as expansion of possibilities and so on (ibid., p. 33). What unites different usages of the word 'Erziehung' is the idea that certain influences bring about certain effects – although there is a wide range of different views about the extent to which the effects that are supposed to be brought about by 'Erziehung' can be contained and controlled (see ibid., chapter 1). This is why Oelkers suggests that 'Erziehung' always entails a certain 'hope' or expectation about its efficacy, despite the fact that 'Erziehung' often fails to achieve what it sets out to achieve (ibid., p. 32) (see also Oelkers 1993), first and foremost because, as discussed earlier in this book, the relationship between 'Erziehung' and its 'effects' is not a causal relationship.

Within the plurality of views about the meaning, content and scope of 'Erziehung', Oelkers identifies three common characteristics of *theories* of 'Erziehung' (see ibid., p. 255). The first is that all theories of 'Erziehung' focus on morality; the second is that they refer to interactions between human beings ('Personen erziehen andere Personen' – persons educate other persons) and the third is that 'Erziehung' has to do with asymmetrical relationships, most notably between adults and children, as well as between teachers and students. Following on from this Oelkers argues that all theories of 'Erziehung' should include the following three aspects: a definition of the *aims* of 'Erziehung', an account of the *process* of 'Erziehung' and a conception of the *object* of 'Erziehung' (ibid., p. 263).

This brief account already shows an important difference between the Anglo-American and the Continental configuration of the field of educational studies, in that in the Continental configuration educational theorizing does not start from 'other' disciplines and their perspectives *on* education, but is depicted as a field in its own right, a field which involves an engagement both with the question of the definition(s) of 'Erziehung' and with theorizing 'Erziehung' through a focus on aims, processes and the object of 'Erziehung'. Oelkers's reconstruction is, of course, not unique. Groothoff (1973), for example, provides a similar definition of 'Erziehung' as encompassing, on the one hand, any help towards the process of becoming a human being ('Menschwerdung') and, on the other hand, any help towards becoming part of the life of society (see Groothoff 1973, p. 73). Whereas on the one hand 'Erziehung' can thus be understood as a function of society – this is, for example, the way in which Wilhelm Dilthey saw 'Erziehung' (see ibid.) – Groothoff emphasizes that in contemporary society 'Erziehung' cannot be confined to adaptation to the existing sociocultural order but also needs to anticipate the independence of thought and action of the ones who are being educated. It must include, in other words, an orientation towards maturity – or, with the much more specific German term which resonates with the English notion of 'autonomy', it must anticipate the 'Mündigkeit' of the ones to be educated.[6]

Against this background – which Groothoff characterizes as a conception of 'Erziehung' that has its roots in the Enlightenment (see also Biesta 2006) – Groothoff argues that a *theory* of 'Erziehung' needs to encompass the following elements: (1) a theory of becoming a human being, (2) a theory of interpersonal interaction, (3) a theory of emancipatory learning, (4) a theory of contemporary social life and its perspectives on the future, (5) a theory of the ends and means of education and their interrelationships and (6) an account of the specific ends and means in the context of the different domains and institutions of 'Erziehung' (ibid., p. 74). Groothoff argues that such a theory can be found in the work of Friedrich Schleiermacher and, to a lesser extent, in the work of Wilhelm Dilthey (ibid., p. 74). Groothoff, writing in 1973, believes that such an encompassing theory of education is no longer possible in our time, not only because the field of 'Erziehung' has become much more complex but also because society has lost confidence in itself. Groothoff therefore presents the field of 'Pädagogik' – understood as the 'science'[7] of 'Erziehung' – as a more fragmented field where individual theorists work on aspects of educational theorizing, rather than that they all engage with all aspects of what is considered to be part of the theory of 'Erziehung'.

---

[6] The distinction Groothoff hints at here maps onto the difference between socialization and subjectification in the three-dimensional model of educational purpose I have introduced earlier in this book.

[7] I put 'science' in quotation marks because the English word 'science' does not entirely translate the meaning of the German notion of 'Wissenschaft', mainly because 'Wissenschaft' encompasses the natural sciences and the humanities.

The discipline of 'Pädagogik'

'Erziehung' is understood as teleological – that is, orientated towards a purpose or 'telos' – and value-laden in that 'Erziehung' always involves aims and ends and therefore always requires decisions about which aims and ends are considered to be desirable. Questions about the right way to educate, in terms of both the means and the ends of education, are therefore of central concern for the practice of education. König (1975) argues that at least up to the beginning of the twentieth century this was also the guiding question for the scientific study of education.[8] The theorists of 'Erziehung' thus explicitly conceived of 'Pädagogik' as a *normative* discipline and saw it as their task to articulate aims for education and develop guidelines for educational practice (see König 1975, p. 34). What characterizes work within this tradition was the ambition to articulate *ultimate* educational aims and, more importantly, educational aims that were considered to be universally valid. König discusses a range of different attempts to articulate such universal aims, for example based on theology, on the philosophy of value (the work of Max Scheler and Nicolai Hartmann), on general moral conventions or on practical philosophy (Herbart). This reveals that 'Pädagogik' not only is confined to the formulation of educational aims but also encompasses the justification of such aims.

This particular conception of 'Pädagogik' – known in the literature as the normative conception of 'Pädagogik' – is often presented as the first phase in the development of the field. Some would even characterize it as a pre-phase, arguing that 'Pädagogik' only came to maturity as a scientific discipline[9] once it had overcome its connection to particular normative systems and schools of thought. This was the central idea in a tradition which became known as 'geisteswissenschaftliche Pädagogik'. The idea of 'Pädagogik' as a 'Geisteswissenschaft' – a hermeneutic science – was initiated by Wilhelm Dilthey. Dilthey argued that there was a fundamental distinction between the study of natural phenomena and the study of social and historical phenomena. While the world of natural phenomena is a world of cause and effect which for that reason is amenable to *explanation*, the socio-historical world is a world in

---

[8] Note that in German the notion of 'scientific' – ' wissenschaftlich – is not confined to the natural sciences.

[9] Note again that 'scientific' should be read in a broader sense than the English idea of science.

which human beings pursue aims and plan actions in order to achieve these aims. The main objective of the study of the socio-historical world should therefore be to clarify the aims people pursue.

This, so Dilthey argued, is not a question of explanation but requires *understanding*. Moreover, such understanding cannot be generated through observation from the 'outside', but needs interpretation and an insider perspective. As education is a thoroughly socio-historical phenomenon, so Dilthey argued, 'Pädagogik' thus has to be conceived as a 'Geisteswissenschaft'. The main task of such a 'geisteswissenschaftliche Pädagogik' is that of the *interpretation* of the practice of education in order to bring about understanding of it from the perspective of everyone involved. Dilthey's design for a 'geisteswissenschaftliche Pädagogik' entailed an explicit rejection of normative 'Pädagogik' – or to be more precise, it entailed a rejection of the ambition of normative 'Pädagogik' to articulate *universal* or *external* educational aims (see ibid., p. 99). For Dilthey the aims of education are always relative to and internal to particular socio-historical configurations. This meant that for Dilthey 'Pädagogik' remained a normative discipline, but one with a hermeneutical structure, aimed at the *clarification* of the aims and ends implicit in particular educational practices rather than with the task to prescribe such aims and ends.

Dilthey's ideas provided the main frame of reference for the development of 'geisteswissenschaftliche Pädagogik' in Germany in the first decades of the twentieth century. Through the efforts of educationalists such as Max Frischeisen-Köhler, Hermann Nohl, Eduard Spranger, Otto-Friedrich Bollnow, Wilhelm Flitner, Erich Weniger and Theodor Litt, 'geisteswissenschaftliche Pädagogik' became the main 'paradigm' for the scientific study of education, not only in Germany – where its influence lasted well into the 1960s (see Wulf 1978, p. 15) – but also in countries directly influenced by the German tradition. 'Geisteswissenschaftliche Pädagogik' retained the idea of 'Pädagogik' as a normative discipline, but whereas normative 'Pädagogik' aimed to articulate *universal* aims for education, 'geisteswissenschaftliche Pädagogik' focused on the articulation of aims that were *relative* to particular educational situations and practices.

'Geisteswissenschaftliche Pädagogik' did not see itself as a theoretical discipline but first and foremost as a practical one: a discipline *of* and *for* educational practice. The relationship between 'Pädagogik' and practice was itself understood in hermeneutical terms: its main task was that of the *clarification* of educational practice with the intention to contribute to the *improvement* of educational practice (see König 1975, p. 112; Wulf 1978, p. 17). The task of clarification not only involved analysis and understanding so as to identify the aims of those acting within a particular educational practice – Dilthey's 'programme' – but should also lead to the development of normative guidelines for educational practice, that is, ideas about the 'right' way to act in the particular situation (see König 1975, p. 118). It is along these lines that 'geisteswissenschaftliche Pädagogik' aimed to contribute to the improvement of educational practices.

Although the theorists of 'geisteswissenschaftliche Pädagogik' rejected the idea of universal educational aims, they did see 'Pädagogik' as inherently normative, aimed at the development of ideas about *right* ways to act in particular educational settings and situations. The normativity of 'geisteswissenschaftliche Pädagogik' was closely connected to what may well be one of the most interesting aspects of 'geisteswissenschaftliche Pädagogik', namely the idea of the *relative autonomy* of the practice of education and of 'Pädagogik' as the science of and for education.

The idea of the relative autonomy of 'Pädagogik' first of all had to do with the intention to liberate 'Pädagogik' from its dependence on ethics and theology (which were two important sources for normative 'Pädagogik') and psychology (which played an important role in Herbart's version of normative 'Pädagogik') so as to be able to establish 'Pädagogik' as an independent academic discipline in its own right (see Wulf 1978, p. 35). To do so, the theorists of 'geisteswissenschaftliche Pädagogik' connected the relative autonomy of 'Pädagogik' to the relative autonomy of educational practice. The key idea here was that 'Pädagogik' had a role to play in protecting the domain of education – and through this the domain of childhood more generally – from claims coming from societal powers such as the church, the state or the economy (see Wulf 1978, pp. 17, 35). The autonomy of 'Pädagogik' as an academic discipline was thus articulated in terms of a particular 'educational' interest which the theorists of 'geisteswissenschaftliche Pädagogik' understood as an interest in the right of the child to a certain degree of self-determination (see ibid., p. 36). The fact that the disciplinary identity of 'geisteswissenschaftliche Pädagogik' was articulated in terms of a particular educational *interest* is a further reason why 'Pädagogik', at least according to the theorists of 'geisteswissenschaftliche Pädagogik', is a normative discipline, albeit one that is open to a plurality of views about what it exactly means to be committed to the autonomy of educational practice and the self-determination of children.

What makes 'geisteswissenschaftliche Pädagogik' interesting for the discussion in this chapter is that it presents a well-defined set of ideas about how and why 'Pädagogik' can be understood as an academic discipline in its own right. This is not to suggest that 'geisteswissenschaftliche Pädagogik' has been the only way in which the field has been organized and conceived, although within the German tradition it still stands out as the first attempt to make 'Pädagogik' into an independent academic discipline rather than one being dependent upon other disciplines (such as psychology) or value systems (such as theology or ethics). Although the heydays of 'geisteswissenschaftliche Pädagogik' are over, partly as a result of the emergence of forms of empirical research and partly as a result of the influence of the critical theory of the Frankfurt School, the particular questions that 'geisteswissenschaftliche Pädagogik' put on the agenda still play an important role in contemporary discussions (see, for example, Oelkers 2001; Benner 2005).

Discussion

The foregoing exploration reveals some interesting differences between the two configurations of the field. It also shows that the questions about disciplines and disciplinarity play an important role in the different ways in which the academic study of education has been conceived and constructed. Whereas in the Anglo-American configuration educational studies is conceived as an inter- or multidisciplinary field, the key ambition of 'geisteswissenschaftliche Pädagogik' was to develop a case for 'Pädagogik' as a discipline in its own right. Whereas Hirst explicitly denied that educational theory can be an autonomous discipline – the reason being that educational theory does not generate any 'unique understanding' about education but relies entirely on the knowledge generated through the 'fundamental' disciplines – the theorists of 'geisteswissenschaftliche Pädagogik' made a strong case for the autonomy of 'Pädagogik'. Interestingly enough they did not argue for the disciplinary autonomy of 'Pädagogik' on the basis of a particular object of study but rather on the basis of a particular *interest*. Whereas the identity of Anglo-American educational studies can therefore be characterized as *objective* in that it is based on a particular object of study ('education'), the identity of 'Pädagogik' might be characterized as *interested* in that it is based on a particular interest.

It is important to note in this context that the idea that the identity of a discipline is based on a normative interest rather than an object of study is not specific for Continental 'Pädagogik'. Although academic disciplines often present themselves in terms of their particular objects of study, it should not be forgotten that a substantial amount of effort is often invested in the processes through which academic disciplines become connected to particular objects of study. It should also not be forgotten that there are at least a number of 'established' academic disciplines that derive their identity more from their interest than from their object of study, such as, for example, the interest in health that characterizes the discipline of medicine or an interest in justice that characterizes the discipline of law.

Although there is, therefore, an important difference between the two configurations of the field – also exemplified in a different social organization of educational studies and 'Pädagogik' – there is at least one remarkable similarity between the two configurations – at least as presented in this chapter – in that both Hirst's notion of educational theory and the conception of 'Pädagogik' in the tradition of 'geisteswissenschaftliche Pädagogik' are in agreement with regard to the fact that the science of education cannot evade normative questions, that is, questions about what education is for and question about what counts as good education. In the tradition of 'geisteswissenschaftliche Pädagogik' the ambition is to generate guidelines about the right way of action in educational practice, just as for Hirst the key idea is that educational theory should generate ideas about 'what ought to be done in educational activities' (Hirst 1966, p. 53).

Another significant difference between the two configurations has to do with the context in which the study of education emerged and developed. The field of educational studies has primarily been developed in the context of teacher education and thus has had a strong connecting with school education. This is quite different in the history of 'Pädagogik' which is not explicitly or exclusively connected to questions of teaching and school education but has a much wider remit which focuses first and foremost on questions of 'Menschwerdung', that is, of becoming human. Whereas this does not in itself explain the difference between the two configurations, it does highlight the fact that the guiding interests in developing the study of education in these different contexts have been different ones.

Although the main aim of this chapter has been to provide an insight into two significantly different configurations of the academic study of education, comparing the two constructions also makes it possible to see what is specific about each construction – which is, of course, far more difficult without a point of comparison. The most striking difference, so I wish to suggest, has to do with the role and status of what we might call educational theory. From a Continental perspective it is remarkable that the idea of education as a discipline in its own right with its own forms of theory and theorizing is almost entirely absent in the Anglo-American construction of the field. This is not merely a historical fact but a situation that continues up to the present day. A 'remarkable' example of this – remarkable, of course, from a Continental perspective – is a recent special issue of the *Oxford Review of Education* (Vol. 35, no 5), edited by Martin Lawn and John Furlong, called 'The Disciplines of Education in the UK: Confronting the Crisis'. While the issue documents the rise and fall of the disciplines in education and, from that angle, paints a rather worrying picture of the status of the disciplines in contemporary educational research in the UK, it still frames the discussion entirely in terms of the Anglo-American configuration. Although it adds a number of disciplines to the 'mix' – alongside contributions from the psychology, sociology, history and philosophy of education, there are also papers on economy, geography and comparative education – it does not raise any questions about the configuration in *itself*, neither when looking at the past nor when envisaging the future. While the focus of the issue is on the situation in the UK, it is remarkable – particularly in an age of internationalization – that the idea of educational theory as something in addition to or alongside contributions from 'other' disciplines and of education as a discipline in itself is never really considered as a possible response to an alleged 'crisis'.

The comparison does, of course, also work in the opposite direction. From this angle we might say that it is remarkable that the Continental configuration is based on the idea of education as an autonomous discipline with its own forms of theory and theorizing. That this idea is perceived as remarkable and, to a certain extent, even 'impossible' from an Anglo-American perspective became clear in a recent exchange that has to do with one of the key arguments provided by the proponents of 'geisteswissenschaftliche Pädagogik' for the idea of 'Pädagogik' as a discipline in its own right. The argument here is that while other disciplines can study educational processes and practices from their own angles, they do not have the devices to capture the reality of education as an *educational* reality. One way to put this predicament is to say that while the psychology of education will ask psychological questions about education, the history of education historical ones, the philosophy of education philosophical ones and the sociology of education sociological ones, the question that remains is who will ask *educational* questions about education. While the idea that there are educational questions to be asked about education that are different from psychological, sociological, historical or philosophical questions about education is a perfectly meaningful idea from within the Continental configuration, a reviewer of an earlier version of this chapter characterized it is totally nonsensical, arguing that it was of the same order as the suggestion that one could ask 'cookery questions about cooking'.

There is, however, one important argument for the suggestion that such an educational perspective is not just possible but is actually necessary for the study of education. This has to do with the question of the object of the study of education. In the Anglo-American configuration it assumed that this object is 'there' and that it is rather easy to identify what education 'is' and where it happens. Yet this is quite misleading, because if one were to walk into a school in order to study the education happening there, one can only do so if one has a certain idea of what *counts* as education. And this is actually more difficult than it may seem, because if one were to say that 'education' is the interaction between teachers and students, one still has to have additional criteria for identifying who the teachers and students are, and will also have to address the question whether *any* interaction between those would count as education or whether only interactions that, for example, aim at certain 'outcomes' would count as education. There are therefore quite a number of questions to be asked, and at some point one has to include normative questions, for example in order to distinguish education (ultimately aimed at the independence of the student) from indoctrination (which would aim at preventing any independent thinking and doing by the student). The study of education, irrespective of the discipline one utilizes, cannot proceed without a definition of education, and such definitions are inevitably normative. This, so I wish to suggest, may well be the blind spot of the Anglo-American configuration, which begins to suggest why bringing the two configurations into a more productive dialogue may be quite urgent.

Five questions for discussion and further consideration

1. Would you classify your research as educational research? What does that mean in light of the ideas presented in this chapter?
2. What is the object of your research? How have you been able to identify this as a researchable object?
3. Which academic disciplines play a role in your research? Which role do they play?
4. Do you agree with Hirst that education cannot be an independent academic discipline?
5. Do you think that it is important for education to claim its own position among other academic disciplines or is this not really relevant?

6

Education, Measurement and Democracy

Educational research that has the ambition to make education better cannot do so through direct intervention into what happens in schools, colleges, universities and other educational settings and practices but has to bear in mind that the practice of education is first and foremost the result of the work of educational practitioners: teachers and other educational professionals. Without those practitioners there is no education, so one could argue that the improvement of education always needs to work 'through' them. Yet there are still two ways in which this can be done – a prescriptive way that assumes that research should tell educational practitioners what they should do and one where research provides educational practitioners with insights and understandings that can play a role in the deliberation and judgements they make in the concrete practices they are working in. Research can, in other words, either reduce or enhance the professional agency of educators and can therefore either enhance the democratic quality of educational professionality or limit or undermine it. In this chapter I explore these wider issues through an analysis of the ways in which the scope for professional judgement and action in education has been transformed – indicating both challenges and opportunities.

Introduction: Education in an age of measurement

In this chapter I explore the impact of the contemporary culture of measurement on education as a professional field. I focus particularly on the democratic dimensions of professionalism, which includes both the democratic qualities of professional action in education itself and the way in which education, as a profession, supports the wider democratic cause. I show how an initial authoritarian conception of professionalism was opened up in the 1960s and 1970s towards more democratic and more inclusive forms of professional action. I then show how, in the wake of the transformation of the welfare state and the rise of neoliberal forms of governing, the democratic dimension of professionalism became distorted. I discuss three distortions, having to do with the position of clients, the nature of accountability and the status of professional knowledge. While at first sight the developments in each of these areas can be seen as furthering the democratization of the professions, I argue that in fact they have eroded the democratic dimension of the professions and show the contribution of the culture of measurement to this erosion process. In the final step of my argument I suggest how a more democratic mode of professional action might be regained and how such a mode of professional action might contribute to wider processes of democratization.

Oscar Wilde's famous contention that nowadays people know the price of everything but the value of nothing – which is offered as a definition of a cynic – seems to capture quite well one of the main problems of the 'age of measurement' (Biesta 2009c; 2010f) in which contemporary education appears to operate. Nowadays there is, after all, an abundance of information about the performance of individual students, groups of students, schools, school districts and even national educational systems as a whole, just as the global measurement industry is trying to pin down the exact 'value' teachers are supposedly adding to all this. But while the performance of all aspects of the education system is measured in much detail and with much precision and statistical sophistication, the question that remains is whether this brings us any closer to an understanding of the value of the processes and practices that are being measured. The question that remains, in other words, is whether what is going on in our age of measurement is getting us any closer to an understanding of what makes education *good* rather than what makes it merely effective or efficient.

This is not just a matter of the *technical validity* of the measurements being made, which concerns the question whether such measurements are measuring what they are supposed to measure. There is the additional and much more urgent question of what I have elsewhere suggested to call the *normative validity* of such measurements (Biesta 2010f). This concerns the question of whether what is being measured actually represents what we value about education, that is, whether it corresponds to our conception of good education. It is here that we can find one of the major problems of the current measurement regime in education. Simply put, it is the question of whether we are measuring what we value, or whether we are valuing what is being measured. We might think of this as an open question, but perhaps it is more accurate to treat it as a diagnosis of what is currently going on in many countries around the world, where we have reached a situation wherein measurement is to a large degree driving education policy and practice without any longer asking whether what is being measured adequately represents a view of good education. One example of this can be found in what is known as 'performativity' (see, for example, Ball 2003). This is the situation where *indicators* of quality are taken as *definitions* of quality. We can see this happening, for example, when reaching a certain position in a league table becomes the strategic target for an organization.

The impact of the measurement regime on contemporary education is at least partly the result of its sheer size – which is why I find it appropriate to speak of a global measurement *industry*. But while size matters, it is also important to note the way in which the measurement industry has managed to bring a wide range of actors with significantly different interests into one network, including researchers, academics, national governments, commercial publishers and supranational organizations such as the OECD and the World Bank, thus creating, as Bruno Latour (1987) has called it, a strong *asymmetry* between those who are inside the network and those who are outside of it. This makes it significantly more difficult, more expensive and more energy- and time-consuming to interrupt and oppose this network with meaningful alternatives, even to the point where the impression may arrive that actually 'there is no alternative'.

There are two further dimensions that matter here: one having to do with the rhetorical dimensions of the discussion and the other with its social psychology. With regard to the first it is important to note that the culture of measurement stems from a complex rationale which combines a number of different discourses and agendas, connected to such notions as accountability, control, transparency, evidence, choice and social justice. The problem at a rhetorical level is that this allows for a 'quick switch' (Charlton 2002) between the different discourses, which makes it more difficult to effectively challenge and criticize the modes of functioning of the measurement regime. Think, for example, of the way in which a critique of measurement as a form of teacher control is rebuffed by playing the social justice card that transparency is needed in order to make sure that everyone has access to good education. Given that different discourses, agendas and interests are at stake, the problem that quickly arises is that it is not clear which ends are supposed to justify which means – or to put it more cynically, it is precisely because of this confused connection between means and ends that people can get away with more than that they should be getting away with.

With regard to the social psychology of the measurement regime the question remains why people are attracted by it or, put differently, why so many people fall for it. Fear plays an important role here. There is first of all the pseudo-security of numbers, stemming from the idea that measurements are objective and can release us from the more difficult task of making judgements. That this security is a pseudo-security is because measurement is ultimately about expressing one thing in terms of another, so that the underlying standard is basically arbitrary and always turns us back to judgement.[1] The measurement industry is also fuelled by a fear of risk and a concomitant desire for control. Here we should not forget, as mentioned earlier in this book, that if we try to control education completely, we turn it into a machinery in which what matters educationally is ultimately squeezed out. And perhaps the most influential driver of the measurement industry is the fear of being left behind. This is the fear that other countries or education systems will, in some respect or on some criteria, do 'better' than we do. The problem here is that one often forgets to ask whether one really would like to be the same as those one is lagging behind to and what the status of the criteria on which some are positioned as being more 'ahead' than others actually is. Should we indeed simply accept that with regard to its education system every country wants to become – and should want to become – like Finland, Singapore or South Korea?

---

[1] Somewhere in his writings John Dewey recounts the story of how, when he was a young boy, they would weigh pigs on the farm. They would put a pig on one end of a scale and stones on the other end until the scale was in balance – and then they would estimate the weight of the stones.

The democratization of the professions

The traditional case for professional autonomy, that is, for the idea that professionals should regulate and control their own work, relies on three assumptions (see, for example, Freidson 1994). The first is that the work of professionals distinguishes itself from many other areas of work in that it is concerned with the promotion of *human well-being*. This already indicates that professionality is not merely technical but always entails a normative dimension. Secondly, it is argued that unlike many other fields of work, professional work relies on *highly specialist knowledge and skills*, which is one of the reasons why the education of the traditional professions (doctors, lawyers and priests) has always taken place in institutions of higher education. Thirdly, it is argued that the work of professionals distinguishes itself from other areas of work because professionals work in *relationships of authority and trust*. These three assumptions constitute, on the one hand, a *definition* of professionalism and therefore appear each time a new area of work seeks to elevate itself to the status of a profession. On the other hand, the assumptions constitute a *justification* for the special status of the professions and for its system of self-regulation.

The traditional configuration of professionalism sees professions as closed and largely inward-looking entities that, although performing important functions for society, in a sense operate at a distance and even isolated from society. In their traditional set-up, professions thus largely operate beyond democratic control, either from clients or from society at large. This is most clearly visible in the fact that professions regulate their own functioning with regard to quality control, entrance to the profession – including the regulation of professional education – and, in case of professional failure and misconduct, also the 'exit' from the profession. This makes professions into powerful entities that exert power both over their own functioning and over important domains of human well-being. The power of professions also helps to understand why relations of authority and trust can easily turn into unjustified exertion of power and even abuse of power.

The democratic deficit of the professions was fundamentally exposed and challenged in the 1960s and 1970s, partly as a result of client and patient emancipation (for example in the medical domain and psychiatry) and partly as a result of changing conceptions of health and mental well-being, for example in alternative medicine and anti-psychiatry (such as the work of R. D. Laing; see, for example, Laing 1960; Laing & Esterson 1964; for medicine, see also Hellín 2002). These developments, which themselves were part of wider protest and emancipation movements at the time (including the student revolts of 1968 and the rise of the anti-education movement in Germany, known as *anti-Pädagogik*; see, for example, Von Braunmühl 1975), particularly exposed the abuse of power within professional relationships and, through this, were aimed at what we might call a democratic redefinition of the relationship between professionals and their clients. To the extent to which, after the Second World War, many professions became more central in the project of the welfare state (see, for example, Björkman 1982), a further shift occurred from a strict orientation on individual clients and their needs towards a wider concern for the common good. This can be seen as a second democratizing impulse where professions increasingly established relationships of democratic accountability with their clients and society more generally.

Three post-democratic distortions

This potted history of the development of professions and professionalism is first of all important in order to make visible how in the 1960s and 1970s a democratization of the traditional configuration of the professions was set into motion, both as a result of a redefinition of the relationship between professionals and their clients and as a result of the redefinition of the relationship between professions and professionals and their societal environment – something that was particularly connected to the role of the professions in emerging welfare states after the Second World War. Understanding these developments is also important, however, in order to grasp the significance of more recent shifts and changes in professional fields such as health care and education which, at first sight, may appear as furthering the case for the democratization of professions but which, on closer inspection, turn out to be undermining the democratic configuration of professional work. In this section I focus on three 'post-democratic distortions': (1) the transformation of clients, patients and also students into customers; (2) the transformation of a democratic conception of accountability into a technical–managerial conception and

(3) the transformation of professional knowledge into 'evidence', linked to the idea of evidence-based practice.

These developments should be understood against the background of the transformation of the welfare state and the rise of neoliberal forms of governance and governing. The transformation of the welfare state – which was partly the result of economic crises such as the oil crisis in the 1970s and partly the result of ideological interventions such as the conservative idea of the small state ('Thatcherism') (see Faulks 1998) – resulted in a shift from an orientation towards social justice and solidarity (the idea of 'the common good') towards a view of the state as a provider of a limited set of public services. What neoliberalism added to this was the redefinition of the state as that of a regulator of the market of public services, no longer concerned with a substantive and hence political definition of the common good but with formal notions such as 'quality', 'choice' and 'the customer always comes first'. As a result, neoliberal governments no longer see themselves as a key actor in the political debate about the definition of the common good but increasingly understand themselves as process managers who, through a regime of standards, measurement and inspection, try to secure the quality of the products on offer. 'Quality' itself is understood in strictly formal terms, that is, as the situation where a particular provision or service meets certain standards, without – as I have already hinted at in the introduction to this chapter – concern for the question of how meaningful those standards actually are. In what way, then, have professional fields been caught up in these developments and how has this distorted their democratic potential?

A first distortion: From client/patient/student to customer

I have indicated earlier that the emancipation of clients, patients and students in the 1960s and 1970s not only exposed the democratic deficit of many professions but also resulted in a transformation of professions and, more specifically, in a transformation of professional relationships. Clients, patients and students literally made their voices heard in order to make clear that they were not just objects of the action and interventions of professionals but subjects in their own right who therefore wanted to be treated as subjects of dialogue and not objects of intervention. From this angle it may seem that the recent trend to refer to clients, patients and students as customers and the tendency to emphasize that in such domains as health care and education professionals must offer what their customers want, are the ultimate steps in the democratization of the professions – one where those at the receiving end, so to speak, are in total control.

But is this indeed the ultimate step in the democratization of the professions? I have reasons to doubt that this is the case, and the main reason has to do with a fundamental difference between economic transactions and professional transactions (see Feinberg 2001). Whereas in economic transactions customers know what they want and would just look for a company that can provide them with what they want for the best possible combination of price and quality, a key aspect of professional relationships is that professionals not just service the needs of their 'clients' but also play a key role in the *definition* of what it is that their clients need. Clients, patients and students, in other words, do not engage with professionals just to get what they already know that they want. Part of the process is precisely to figure what it is that clients actually need. As Feinberg (2001) explains, we go to the doctor because we have a headache, but we expect that the doctor figures out what the headache is an indication of and what can be done to get rid of it. This already suggested that the redefinition of clients, patients and students as customers is based on a fundamental misunderstanding of what professional practices are and what they are about.

A clear example of what is at stake here can be found in the domain of education and upbringing. If parents were only to give their children what they say they want, and never raise the question – for themselves but also in dialogue with their children – whether what their children say they want is actually good for them, it is quite likely that their children will turn into spoilt brats who remain slaves of their desires rather than that they are in a position where they can have a mature perspective on their desires in order to judge which of their desires are actually desirable. It is here that we can locate the specific responsibility of educators, and a similar argument can be made in relation to most if not all professions: just giving clients what they say they want may be utterly unprofessional. Doctors are not just there to give their patients just what they want, but they have a key role in finding out what might be wrong with the patient in order then to propose possible treatments. Patients do have a voice in all of this – for example with regard to questions concerning the risks and benefits of a particular treatment – but this is always to be understood as a *dialogue* between the experiential expertise of the patient and the professional expertise of the doctor. It is not a process where the doctor simply sells what the patient wants to have.

For precisely these reasons then, the redefinition of clients, patients and students as customers is not a further step in the democratization of professional work and professional relationships but rather a development that subverts the unique contribution professionals make. The reason for this lies in the fact that the redefinition of clients, patients and students as customers only puts the authoritarian relationship on its head by giving all the power to the customer. What it fails to see is that real emancipation and real democratization require a *redefinition of the relationship* between professionals and their clients where both play a distinctive role in a dialogical process of needs-definition – it is *not just a reversal of the traditional set-up*.

A second distortion: From democratic to technical–managerial accountability

A second distortion has to do with the way in which a democratic conception of accountability has been replaced by a technical–managerial one. In a democratic conception of accountability professionals are accountable for the quality of their professional action in a direct dialogical relationship with their stakeholders (clients, patients, students and ultimately society as a whole). In a technical–managerial conception of accountability, however, the focus is no longer on the quality of professional action. Rather professionals are held accountable for the degree in which their actions meet certain standards. The role of the state in this set-up, as already alluded to, is to guarantee the quality of the 'product' delivered by the professions. But it does not do so by engaging in a substantial political discussion about what, for example, good mental health care or good education ought to be, but by formulating standards and by initiating systems of inspection and control that need to make sure that professionals' services meet the standards. The question of the normative validity of the standards is hardly ever discussed, or is brushed aside as 'ideological'. What happens as a result of this is the creation of a gap between professionals (redefined as providers) and their clients (redefined as customers). In this gap we find a whole machinery of often privatized quality controllers and inspectors, which means that the accountability relationships between professionals and their clients are no longer direct but have become *indirect*.

This is another example of what, at first sight, seems to further the democratization of the professions but what, on closer inspection, turns out to be an erosion of the possibility for substantial democratic dialogue between professions/professionals and their clients. In her Reith lectures on accountability Onara O-Neill (O'Neill 2002) has shown in much detail what goes wrong here. She reveals two important shifts in the rise of the technical–managerial approach to accountability. The first has to do with a shift with regard to the different parties involved in accountability processes. She writes:

> In theory the new culture of accountability and audit makes professionals and institutions more accountable to the public. This is supposedly done by publishing targets and levels of attainment in league tables, and by establishing complaint procedures by which members of the public can seek redress for any professional or institutional failures. But underlying this ostensible aim of accountability to the public the real requirements are for accountability to regulators, to departments of government, to funders, to legal standards. The new forms of accountability impose forms of central control – quite often indeed a range of different and mutually inconsistent forms of central control. (O'Neill 2002)

A second shift has to do with definitions of quality. Here she writes:

> In theory again the new culture of accountability and audit makes professionals and institutions more accountable *for good performance*. This is manifest in the rhetoric of improvement and raising standards, of efficiency gains and best practice, of respect for patients and pupils and employees. But beneath this admirable rhetoric the real focus is on performance indicators chosen for ease of measurement and control rather than because they measure accurately what the quality of performance is. (O'Neill 2002; emphasis in original)

O'Neill's observations thus clearly show the difference between a democratic and a technical–managerial approach to accountability and the slippery slope between the two.

A third distortion: From professional knowledge to evidence-based practice

The third arena in which the democratization of professionalism has been distorted has to do with the way in which professional judgement in a range of different professional domains is increasingly being replaced with or pushed out by a demand for an evidence-based approach (see also Chapter 3). The idea here is that professional action can only become really professional if it is no longer based on the singular insights (or according to some, subjective opinions) of professionals, but when it becomes based upon secure scientific knowledge about 'what works', And the claim is that the *only* way in which we can be certain that a professional intervention 'works' is by means of randomized controlled trials – in the literature known as the 'golden standard' – which has even led to situations where professionals are prevented from doing anything *unless* there is positive evidence that their interventions will work.

While proponents of evidence-based approaches claim that professional fields such as education, social work and care can be improved dramatically if they opt for the evidence-based approach which, so it is claimed, has been the main driver of progress in such fields as agriculture and medicine (see for this particular argument Slavin 2002), there are a number of reasons why the idea of 'what works' is actually not that easily incorporated. One key issue is that in domains such as care and education – although this ultimately also holds for agriculture and medicine – the question can never simply be about 'what works' but always needs to be phrased as the question 'What works for what?' The point is that any idea of 'working' always needs to be understood in relation to the aim or aims of professional action in a particular field. This already shows that the question of 'what works' can, at most, be relevant with regard to the *means* of professional action but not with regard to the *ends*.

The more important point with regard to the question whether the idea of an evidence-based approach makes sense in domains of professional action has to do with the fact that all professional action takes place in what Aristotle already distinguished as the domain of the 'variable' (see Aristotle 1980), the domain of actions and *possible* consequences and not the domain of the 'eternal', that is, the domain of secure cause–effect relationships. One reason for this lies in the fact that professional action takes place between human beings who never appear just as objects of intervention – which also shows that the language of intervention is actually quite misleading – but always also as subjects in their own right. In the domain of the variable, research can therefore at most provide us with information about *possible* relationships between actions and consequences. But research can never guarantee that relationships between actions and consequences that were found in the past will appear in exactly the same way in the present. While research therefore can tell us what in a concrete situation and under specific circumstances *has worked* in the past, it can never tell us what *will work* in the present or the future. Next to the need to make judgements about the ends of professional action, we therefore also always need judgement about how to act – which is a judgement about the application of general and decontextualized knowledge to concrete situations and singular cases. Scientific evidence can replace neither judgements about how to act nor judgements about the aims and ends of professional action – and where we find claims that it can or should, we have an example of *positivism*, where the means are defining the ends, rather than that we are in a position to define the ends of our actions ourselves.

The call, and in some cases even the blunt demand to work in an evidence-based way, thus appears as an attempt to eradicate professional judgement with regard to the 'how' and the 'what for' of professional action from the domain of professionalism. It seeks to transform professions into abstract 'machines' in which reflection and judgement are seen as a weakness rather than as an essential part of it, thus completely misunderstanding what a practice such as education actually is (see also Chapter 4). This shows how the call for an evidence-based approach is not a deepening of the knowledge and judgement of professionals but rather an attempt to overrule such knowledge and judgement. In precisely this sense the evidence-based approach is another erosion of the democratic dimension of professionalism and hence another post-democratic distortion.

The role of measurement

If the foregoing provides us with an insight into the ways in which recent developments in professional fields such as education are hindering rather than enhancing their democratic potential, there is the additional question of how the culture of measurement is contributing to this. With regard to this question I wish to make two observations. First, I wish to highlight that central to each distortion is an apparent need for data, information and measurement. After all, to give customers what they want and to give them choice and value for money, they seem to need data about the quality of the products on offer. Also, to hold professionals accountable for the quality of their performance there is an apparent need for data about the degree in which their work meets preset standards. And in order to make professional activity evidence based there is a need for information about what works, particularly data that reveal the links between 'interventions' and 'outcomes'.

This shows that the culture of measurement has played and continues to play a key role in the post-democratic transformation of the professions in that these transformations *require* data and measurement. At the very same time, the availability of data, information and measurement *reinforces* these particular distortions rather than that they work against them. After all, once there are data available about the performance of individuals, groups or systems, it becomes increasingly difficult not to look at the data. Similarly, once there are data about the performance of individuals, groups or systems, it is difficult not to include them in any accountability exercise. And once some kind of apparent 'evidence' has been constructed about particular practices and ways of working, it becomes again difficult not to make use of it. The availability of data, information and measurement, to put it differently, is seductive and difficult to resist – which reveals another dimension of the social psychology of the culture of measurement and provides a further explanation for its attractiveness and 'force'. Are there any options for 'fighting back' and for reclaiming democratic professionalism? I wish to make three suggestions.

Reclaiming a space for democratic professionalism

The first thing that needs to be done – to which I have contributed in this chapter – is to challenge, interrupt and resist the redefinition of the professions, particularly with regard to the three distortions I have analyzed above: the redefinition of the client/patient/student as a customer, the replacement of democratic accountability with technical–managerial accountability and the attempt to replace professional knowledge with evidence about 'what works'. In each case it is particularly important to show that these developments are based on a misunderstanding of what professional work is about and what the nature of professional practices such as education actually is.

Secondly it is important to expose the democratic deficit of these developments, that is, to show that in spite of what may seem to be the case at first sight and in spite of the claims being made, they are actually undermining and eroding the development of more democratic ways of working in professional fields such as health care and education. For this it is important to highlight – as I have done – that democratization of the professions is not a matter of reversing the positions of the involved parties, that is, just turning authoritarian relationships on their head. It rather requires the establishment of new relationships between professionals and their clients – relationships of dialogue where both can contribute their particular experience and expertise, acknowledging that the experience and expertise of each of the parties involved (professionals and clients) are different and complementary, and that the differing contributions from all are needed in order to transform authoritarian professional relationships into democratic ones.

To resist post-democratic transformations of dimensions of professional work and to insist on the need to transform relationships rather than just reverse them often mean that one finds oneself defending ideas and positions that, at first sight, may look outdated. For example, to argue against the 'learnification' of education (Biesta 2010f), that is, against a conception of education that puts the learner at the centre and sidelines the teacher, and, in response to these developments make a case for the importance of teaching and the teacher (Biesta 2012, 2017b), is often perceived as a step back rather than a step forward. So, it needs careful argumentation to show that the turn towards the learner and away from the teacher is actually an inadequate response to authoritarian forms of teaching as control, as it only reverses the position of the student and teacher, rather than that it seeks to transform the nature of their relationship. Similarly, to argue that education should be understood as value based rather than evidence based, as I have done earlier in this book, is often perceived as a return to a pre-scientific age rather than as an attempt to show that science – in the form of evidence or otherwise – can never do away with the need for deliberation and judgement.

The overarching task in all this is to resist technicist conceptions of professionalism, such as the reduction of the role of the teacher to that of a technician who just implements and executes pre-specified routines (see also

Leaton Gray 2007), and to provide a viable and robust alternative. Throughout this chapter such a different conception of professionalism has been emerging. In the final section I wish to highlight the key dimensions of this conception of professionalism, taking my examples from teaching. I will also show how this conception of professionalism connects professional work to the idea of democracy, thus outlining a conception of the democratic professional and democratic professionalism.

Conceptualizing the democratic professional

I wish to suggest that professional work is characterized by three aspects: (1) an orientation towards the 'telos' of the practice, (2) engagement with processes of needs-definition and (3) engagement with the transformation of power into authority. Let me clarify what I have in mind.

I started this chapter with the traditional definition of professionality. There I argued that professions are characterized by an orientation towards human well-being. This already reveals that professional action is never merely technical; that is, it is never just concerned with the production of a particular effect or a particular outcome but rather is orientated towards the realization of the 'telos' of the particular practice. Although we might translate the Greek word 'telos' into 'aim', it is more appropriate to translate it into 'purpose', as the 'telos' of a practice refers to that which the practice seeks to promote in a more general sense. In health care the 'telos' is the promotion of health; in the legal professions it is the promotion of justice; whereas in education we might say that it is the promotion of 'educatedness', which, for example, can be characterized as the promotion of the cognitive and moral independence of students.

Whereas the aims of professional action are the more concrete achievements or results professionals seek to bring about, the purpose or 'telos' of a practice refers to that which gives a practice its meaning, identity and sense of direction. This is why it is a mistake to think of teaching, for example, simply as the production of measurable 'learning outcomes'. While there may be a place for this in teaching, it can never be the be all and end all of education but needs to be considered in relation to the wider 'telos' of education. The question as to what the 'telos' of education should be, is a question that cannot simply be settled once and for all, but rather requires ongoing reflection and deliberation among interested parties, for example with regard to the criteria of what would count as an educated person. Answering this question is never a matter of facts but always involves normative preferences and choices. This already is one important reason why teaching, just as all other professions that are constituted by a 'telos', has to be understood as a normative profession, not just a technical one (on the idea of normative professionalism, see Kunneman 1996).

The second characteristic of the conception of professionalism I am putting forward in this chapter concerns the fact that professionals do not simply service the needs of their clients but play a key role in defining those needs. Whereas in the traditional conception of professionality this was seen as the sole responsibility of the professional – the idea of 'the doctor knows best' – in democratic conceptions of professionality this is understood as a dialogical process in which professionals and their clients both have something to contribute. It is important to bear in mind that professionals and their clients occupy different roles and carry different responsibilities in this relationship.

In education the process of needs-definition takes the form of introducing a distinction between what children and students (and often also their parents) desire and what can be considered as desirable for them – with regard to both their individual lives and the lives they live with others. This is, for example, how the French educationalist Philippe Meirieu (2008) characterizes the core 'interest' of education, namely as a process where we try to release children from their desires by opening up a distinction between what they desire and what might be desirable for them. Initially educators play a key role in answering this question for the children and students they are responsible for. But over time this question – 'Is what I desire also desirable for me?' – should become a question children and students ask about their own desires. At that point one could say that they have developed a 'grown up' perspective on their desires and are no longer simply dominated by them. This suggests that educational processes are not merely affirmative in that they do not simply accept the desires of children and students but always entail moments of interruption where such desires are examined and questioned. To initiate such interruptions, to ask students which of their desires are actually desirable for them, is again not a factual matter but a thoroughly normative endeavour that requires judgements about which desires are to be valued.

The third aspect of the conception of professionality I am putting forward in this chapter has to do with the fact that professional relationships are characterized by authority. It is very important here to make a distinction between power and authority, and hence between authoritarian relationships and relationships of authority. Whereas authoritarian relationships are about one-sided power and control, relationships of authority are relationships of what we might call 'accepted' or 'justified' power. This first of all highlights that authority is fundamentally *relational* (see Bingham 2008). It is not something one person can possess and can exercise over another person but has to be understood as something that 'circulates' in relationships and thus requires 'support' from all parties in the relationship. It is not, for example, that teachers automatically have authority over their students, but they can, in the development of their mutual relationships, be given authority by their students – they can be 'authorized' by their students, so to speak. The transformation of (relationships of) power into (relationships of) authority is one of the key dynamics of all professional relationships if they seek to operate in a democratic rather than in an authoritarian way.

To think of professions in terms of their 'telos', in terms of needs-definition and in terms of the transformation of power into authority outlines a notion of professionality that is quite different from the direction in which the current culture of measurements seeks to steer professional fields such as education. Moreover, to think of these dimensions in dialogical rather than one-sided terms highlights the way in which professions can operate democratically rather than that they become dominated by the quasi-democracy of markets, customers and standards. What is interesting about this way of understanding what democratic professionality is about, is that the aspects of 'telos', needs-definition and authority can actually also be seen as defining characteristics of democracy itself.

As I have argued elsewhere in more detail (see, for example, Biesta 2013a), democracy is not to be understood as something 'natural' but rather as a historical invention and intervention, that is, a way of conducting our collective lives based on a commitment to a set of specific values, namely those of equality, liberty and solidarity. As Chantal Mouffe has argued, these values constitute the democratic sphere, albeit that the interpretation of what these values actually stand for has to be ongoing (see Mouffe 2000). This suggests that (the practice of) democracy is itself constituted by a 'telos' that gives it distinctiveness and meaning. A second important point is that, unlike what many seem to think, democracy is not about choice. It is not about the simple expression of one's preferences and the counting of preferences in order then to give all power to the majority. Democracy is rather to be understood as a process in which the 'wants' and desires of individuals and groups are brought into collective deliberation in order to figure out which of those wants and desires can legitimately be 'carried' by the collective. This is far from an arithmetical process, but a truly transformative and also truly educative one, which actually can be understood as a process of collective needs-definition. One could say that the outcome of such processes of deliberation establishes what should have authority in our collective lives. In this regard we can say that democracy itself is characterized by the transformation of power into authority.

Looking at democracy in this way reveals a structural resemblance between the ways in which the democratic professional works and the way in which democracy itself operates, which suggests that the democratization of the professions along these lines is not only relevant for the 'internal' democratic quality of professional fields but may also provide important opportunities for practising and experiencing the wider dynamics of democracy. In this regard democratic professions perform an important contribution to wider processes of societal democratization.

Concluding remarks

In this chapter I have explored the impact of the culture of measurement on professional fields such as education. I have done this through an analysis of the transformation of professions in light of the decline of the welfare state and the rise of neoliberal forms of governing and governance. I have shown that measurement plays an important role in these transformations – transformations that seek to push professions into the direction of standards-driven, evidence-based service providers. Whereas at first sight the transparency and accountability and customer orientation that come with this reconfiguration of the professions may look like a further democratization of the professions, I have shown that these developments actually imply an erosion of their democratic potential. It is against this background that I have outlined the contours of a different conception of professionality in which an orientation towards the 'telos' of the profession, an engagement with needs-definition and the transformation of power relations into relationships of authority are central. Such a democratic conception of professionality provides a starting point for reclaiming what professions such as education operating in a democratic society ought to be about. It provides a starting point, in other words, for a robust and reasoned response against the current erosion of the democratic potential of professional work in the age of measurement.

Five questions for discussion and further consideration

1. Research nowadays makes an important contribution to the culture of measurement. Where does your research sit in relation to this?
2. What do you see as the benefits of treating students as customers? And where do you see problems?
3. Are there particular individuals or groups you seek to serve with your research? If so, how do you see your role vis-à-vis them?
4. Can you articulate where and how educational professionals figure in your research?
5. Could your research, the way in which it is conducted and the ways in which it is communicated, contribute to wider processes of democratization? How? Should it?

7

Knowledge Reconsidered

The question of knowledge is an important one for research – and hence an important one for researchers – not least because many would argue that the prime function of research is to generate knowledge. One could also argue that knowledge is the main vehicle through which research interacts with and seeks to contribute to educational practice, although we have already seen that there are different contributions research can make and that different 'knowledges' and notions of knowledge are at stake here. The distinction between a technical and a cultural role for research is particularly important here, as well as the question of the relationship between knowledge and (educational) action. While educational researchers should be mindful that they are not philosophers and therefore should not have the ambition to resolve ongoing discussions about the nature of knowledge and its possible relationships to action and reality, it is important that research are knowledgeable about these questions, perhaps most of all in order to account for the possibilities and limitations of the knowledge claims they make based on their research. The focus in this chapter is on John Dewey's reflections on the nature of knowledge and its relationship to action, in education and life more generally. His approach is particularly interesting because of its rather effective critique of overblown expectations about what research can achieve.

Introduction: Epistemology and the mind-world scheme

In many philosophical discussions about knowledge it is assumed that the central problem to be solved is that of how the human mind can acquire knowledge of a world outside of itself. Robert Nozick put the challenge most succinctly when he asked whether we can ever know that we are *not* a brain suspended in a vat full of liquid, wired to a computer which is feeding our current experiences (see Nozick 1981, pp. 161–71). Nozick is part of a long tradition in which the nature of knowledge is examined from a *sceptical* point of view, that is by starting from the assumption that knowledge may *not* be possible because we may not be able to get 'outside' of our own mind. The first philosopher to place scepticism at the heart of modern epistemology was René Descartes. In the *Second Meditation* he used the 'method of doubt' to arrive at the conclusion that although we can doubt everything, we cannot, when doing so, doubt that we are engaged in a process of doubting. Whereas this provided Descartes with certainty about the existence of the thinking self, it did *not* provide any certainty about the existence of a world *beyond* our experience, and this issue has troubled modern epistemology ever since. It eventually led David Hume to the conclusion that the existence of an external world of enduring objects is a 'very useful hypothesis' but not something that can ever be proven.

What unites the ideas of Nozick, Descartes and Hume is their reliance on a dualistic view of reality. They assume that reality consists of two totally different 'substances', mind and matter, and that the question of knowledge has to begin with the mind in order then to ask how the mind can get in touch with the material world 'outside' of itself. The dualism between mind and matter has not only set the agenda for modern epistemology by giving it the task to answer the question how the mind can get 'in touch' with the world (see, for example, Dancy 1985) – which is one reason why epistemology cannot be a neutral arbiter in discussions about knowledge, as it is itself 'tainted' by very specific assumptions. The dualism between mind and matter has also provided the framework for the distinction between objectivity and subjectivity and, related to this, for distinctions such as between absolutism and relativism, between realism and idealism and so on. After all, on the basis of the dualism between knowing subjects and objects to be known, knowledge can be objective if it depicts how objects are in themselves, whereas, if this is considered not to be possible, then the only other option is for knowledge to be subjective, that is, produced by the activities of the human mind.

The implications of this way of thinking go well beyond 'technical' questions about knowledge. Many recent discussions about culture, ethics, morality, science, rationality and even Western civilization appear to be informed by the idea that the only choice we have is between the two options presented in the 'mind-world scheme'. More importantly, many participants in these discussions seem to fear that if we give up objectivity, the only thing left is chaos. Richard Bernstein (1983, p. 18) aptly refers to this as the 'Cartesian Anxiety', the idea that *either* there is 'a fixed foundation for our knowledge' *or* we cannot escape 'the forces of darkness that envelop us with madness, with intellectual and moral chaos'.

The mind-world scheme does indeed only offer two options: objectivity or subjectivity. The crucial question, however, is not which option to choose. The far more important question is whether the mind-world scheme is *itself* inevitable or whether it is possible to think about knowledge and reality in a different way, starting from different assumptions. John Dewey's theory of knowing does precisely this. It offers an understanding of knowing that does *not* start from what he saw as the 'impossible question' as to how 'a knower who is purely individual or "subjective", and whose being is wholly psychical and immaterial ... and a world to be known which is purely universal or "objective", and whose being is wholly mechanical and physical' can ever reach each other (Dewey 1911, p. 441). Instead, Dewey put forward a framework which starts with *interactions* – or as he later preferred to call it, *transactions* – taking place in nature and in which nature itself is understood as 'a moving whole of interacting parts' (Dewey 1929, p. 232). This is Dewey's self-confessed 'Copernican turn', in which '(t)he old center was mind' while '(t)he new center is indefinite interactions' (Dewey 1929, p. 232). The key concept in this Copernican turn is 'experience'.

The transactional theory of knowing

While *transaction* refers to interactions taking place in nature more generally, *experience* refers to the transactions of *living* organisms and their environments. What is distinctive about these transactions is that they constitute a *double* relationship.

> The organism acts in accordance with its own structure, simple or complex, upon its surroundings. As a consequence, the changes produced in the environment react upon the organism and its activities. The living creature

undergoes, suffers, the consequences of its own behavior. This close connection between doing and suffering or undergoing forms what we call experience. (Dewey 1920, p. 129)

Experience is therefore the way in which living organisms are implicated in their environment. Contrary to what is suggested in the mind-world scheme, Dewey thus argues that experience is not 'a veil that shuts man off from nature' but rather 'a means of penetrating continually further into the heart of nature' (Dewey 1925, p. 15).

Dewey saw knowing as the mode of experience that in some way 'supports' action. It is concerned with grasping the *relationship* between our actions and their consequences. It is because of this that knowing can help us to get more control over our actions, at least more than in the case of blind trial and error. It is important to see that 'control' here does not mean complete mastery but the ability to intelligently plan and direct our actions. This ability is first of all important in those situations in which we are not sure how to act – which is expressed in one of Dewey's definitions of knowing as having to do with 'the transformation of disturbed and unsettled situations into those more controlled and more significant' (Dewey 1929, p. 236). Knowing is also important in order to achieve more control, a more intelligent approach in the other domains of experience, which is expressed in Dewey's claim that knowing 'facilitates control of objects for purposes of non-cognitive experience' (Dewey 1929, p. 79).

The framework for Dewey's theory of knowing lies in his theory of action, the outlines of which he developed early on in his career in a landmark paper called 'The Reflex Arc Concept in Psychology' (Dewey 1896). One way to summarize Dewey's theory of action is to say that it amounts to *a theory of experimental learning* if, that is, we think of learning as the way in which living organisms interactively 'adapt' to their environments (which in itself is a rather truncated conception of learning, of course; on this, see Biesta 2013b). Dewey characterizes living organisms – including human organisms – as capable of establishing and maintaining a dynamic coordination with their environment. Through this process the predispositions – or 'habits' as Dewey preferred to call them – of the organism become more focused and more specific, more attuned to ever-changing environing conditions, which is another way of saying that through the tentative, experimental way in which living organisms maintain coordinated transaction with their environment they *learn*. This learning, however, is *not* the acquisition of information about how the world 'out there' is. It is a learning process through which living organisms acquire a complex and flexible set of predispositions for action.

On this view, learning is therefore basically a process of trial and error and in one sense this is indeed how Dewey argues that living organisms learn. But there is a difference between blind trial and error and what Dewey called 'intelligent action'. The difference has to do with the intervention of thinking, which he defines as 'dramatic rehearsal (in imagination) of various competing possible lines of action' (Dewey 1922, p. 132). The choice for a specific line of action should be understood as 'hitting in imagination upon an object which furnishes an adequate stimulus to the recovery of overt action' (Dewey 1922, p. 134). Whether this choice will actually lead to coordinated transaction will only become clear when the organism actually acts. This is why thinking can never guarantee that our actions will result in coordinated transactions. But what it can do is make the process of choosing more intelligent than would be the case with 'blind' trial and error.

In Dewey's view the question of knowledge – or to be more precise, the issue of knowing – arises 'because of the appearance of incompatible factors within the empirical situation. (...) Then opposed responses are provoked which cannot be taken simultaneously in overt action, and which accordingly can be dealt with, whether simultaneously or successively, only after they have been brought into a plan of organized action' (Dewey 1916, p. 326). The problem here is one of the *meaning* of the situation – and for Dewey 'situation' always refers to organism and environment in transaction. The only way to solve the problem in an *intelligent* manner and not by simple trial and error is by means of a systematic inspection of the situation. On the one hand, we need to identify and state the problem. On the other hand, we need to develop suggestions for addressing the problem, for finding a way to act and hence to find out what the meaning of the situation actually is. While thought or reflection must play an important part in this process, they will, in themselves, not result in knowledge. It is only when action follows that the value of both the analysis of the problem and the suggested solution can be established. For Dewey, therefore, we need overt action in order to determine the worth and validity of our reflective considerations. Otherwise we have, at most, a hypothesis about the problem and a hypothesis about its possible solution.

This means that in order to get knowledge we need action. But although action is a necessary condition for knowledge, it is not a sufficient one. We also need thinking or reflection. It is the *combination* of reflection and action which leads to knowledge. From this it follows that knowing, the acquisition of knowledge, is not something which takes place somewhere deep down inside the human mind. Knowing is itself an activity; it is 'literally something which we do' (Dewey 1916, p. 367). The meaning which emerges from the restoration of coordinated action is a meaning 'which is contemporaneously aware of meaning something beyond itself' (Dewey 1906, p. 113). This 'beyond' is not simply present or will not simply become present in the future. It will *only* become present 'through the intervention of an operation' (Dewey 1906, pp. 113–14), that is, through what we *do*. A potato becomes edible when we cook it, so after the intervention of the act of cooking – and perhaps we can say, after the discovery that when we cook potatoes we can eat them – the potato means something different in our field of action – it has become 'potentially edible food'.

Therefore, when experience is 'cognitional', as Dewey puts it, it means that we perceive something as meaning-something-else-which-we-will-experience-when-we-act-in-a-specific-way. It is along these lines that knowledge is intimately connected to the possibility of control. 'In knowledge', Dewey argued, 'causes become means and effects become consequences, and thereby things having meaning' (Dewey 1929, p. 236). Knowledge has, in other words, to do with *inference*: a reaction to something which is distant in time or place. Because inference is a step into an unknown future, it is a precarious journey. Inference always involves uncertainty and risk. A stone, Dewey argued, can only react to stimuli of the present, not of the future, and for that reason cannot make mistakes. Since inference entails the possibility of mistake, it introduces truth and falsity into the world.

Experience, reality and knowledge

One important implication of Dewey's transactional definition of experience is that it puts an end to the idea that it is only through knowledge that we can obtain a hold on reality. For Dewey all modes of experience are equally real, since they are all modes of the transaction of living organisms and their environments. From this Dewey concluded that 'things – anything, everything, in the ordinary or non-technical use of the term "thing" – are what they are experienced as' (Dewey 1905, p. 158). This first of all means that everyone's experience is equally real. It also implies that what is experienced is itself real. If someone is frightened by a noise, so Dewey's argument is, then that noise *is* fearsome. This claim must be understood transactionally. If someone is frightened by a sound, then the fear is the immediate response of the organism. The sound *is* frightening because the organism reacts to the sound as being-a-frightening-sound. This implies, however, that *being*-frightened is not the same as knowing-that-one-is-frightened. Knowing what *caused* the fearsome noise is a different experience. While the latter experience may be *more true* than the former, it is in Dewey's view not more *real*. 'The question of truth is not as to whether Being or Non-Being, Reality or mere Appearance is experienced, but as to the *worth* of a certain concretely experienced thing' (Dewey 1905, p. 163; emphasis in original). One important implication of this is that experience in itself does not provide us with any knowledge. Dewey rejected, in other words, the view that experience provides us with elementary 'bits' of knowledge which, when put together in a systematic of logical manner, result in knowledge.[1]

For Dewey the difference between experience and knowledge is that knowledge is concerned with the *occurrence* of experience. The 'office' of knowledge signifies a search 'for those relations upon which the *occurrence* of real qualities and values depends' (Dewey 1929, p. 83; emphasis in original). In this respect knowledge is intimately and necessarily connected with action, because – and this is the most crucial point in Dewey's theory of knowing – the discovery of the conditions and consequences of experience 'can take place *only* by modifying the given qualities in such ways that *relations* become manifest' (Dewey 1929, p. 84; emphasis added). The shift from understanding knowledge as being concerned with the world 'as it is' to understanding knowledge as being concerned with *conditions and consequences* is a very important element of Dewey's approach. It represents a shift from a concern

---

[1] The latter view was the one put forward by logical positivism and, although philosophically discredited, still lives on in the idea that knowledge acquisition is an inductive process starting from the collection of 'basic facts' and working 'upwards' towards general statements (see Ayer 1959; Achinstein & Barker 1969).

with things as they are to a concern with 'the history to which a given thing belongs' (Dewey 1925, p. 243). It is a shift from 'knowing as an aesthetic enjoyment of the properties of nature as a world of divine art, to knowing as a means of secular control – that is, a method of purposefully introducing changes which will alter the direction of the course of events' (Dewey 1929, p. 81). This implies that for Dewey knowledge is concerned with the relations between actions and consequences. This introduces the dimension of *time* into Dewey's theory of knowing – a reason for arguing that Dewey has a temporal conception of knowing.

Dewey's approach also has implications for how we understand the objects of knowledge. Whereas in the dualistic approach the objects of knowledge are seen as 'things' that exist in a world 'out there' and are there for us to discover and depict, Dewey's transactional view sees the objects of knowledge as the *outcomes* of processes of inquiry. Since the habits we acquire through such processes provide us with more specific predispositions for action, habits in a sense embody the ways in which our environment becomes more meaningful for us. The experimental transformation of organism–environment transactions transforms the environment in which and through which we act into what Dewey referred to as 'a figured framework of objects' (Dewey 1922, p. 128). This is the reason why Dewey referred to objects of perception not as things but as 'events with meaning' (Dewey 1925, p. 240).

In the case of spoken language, it is relatively easy to see that words – or 'sound events' – do not have a meaning of their own, but that they have *become* meaningful over time. It is far more difficult to draw the same conclusion with respect to physical objects, such as chairs, tables, trees, stones, hills and flowers, 'where it seems as if the union of intellectual meaning with physical fact were aboriginal' (Dewey 1933, p. 231). Yet chairs and tables are as much events with meaning as words are (for a similar line of thought, see Bloor 1983, in his discussion of Wittgenstein's social theory of knowledge). And their meaning has a strictly transactional origin, in that it has to be understood as the outcome of the specific ways in which successful relationship between our actions and their consequences have been established over time. It is not, therefore, that through a process of inquiry we can find out what the possible meanings of, for example, a chair are. Rather, a chair specifies a particular way in which the transaction with the environment has become meaningful. It is for this reason that Dewey argued that we should think of objects as tools. 'The character of an object is like that of a tool (...); it is an order of determination of sequential changes terminating in a foreseen consequence' (Dewey 1925, p. 121).[2]

The final element of Dewey's theory of knowing has to do with the question of truth. We have already seen that for Dewey there is no sense in asking about the truth of our immediate experience. Immediate experience simply is what it is. Truth and falsity only enter the scene when we raise questions about the *meaning* of experience.

> Truth and falsity are not properties of any experience or thing, in and of itself or in its first intention; *but of things where the problem of assurance consciously enters in. Truth and falsity present themselves as significant facts only in situations in which specific meanings are intentionally compared and contrasted with reference to the question of worth, as to the reliability of meaning'* (Dewey 1906, p. 118; emphasis in original)

Truth and falsity are therefore not concerned with things as such, but with the *relationship* between our experience of a thing on the one hand and our possible actions or responses on the other. This not only means that 'truth' is always contextual and related to action but also means that truth is itself *temporal*. Truth does not refer to an alleged correspondence between a proposition and reality. It has to do with the correspondence between *suggested* meaning and *realized* meaning, that is, meaning 'put into practice'. 'The agreement, correspondence, is between purpose, plan, and its own execution, fulfilment' (Dewey 1907, p. 84).

This does not mean that truth becomes disconnected from reality. The contrary is the case, not only because of the transactional framework that informs Dewey's theory of knowing but also because of the *indispensable* role of action in the process that results in knowledge. The upshot of this is that knowledge is not a passive registration of reality 'out there'. Our intervention, our action, is a crucial, necessary and constitutive part of knowledge. In this sense we can say that knowledge is always a human construction just as the objects of knowledge are. But it does *not* mean that anything is possible. We always intervene in an existing course of events and although our intervention introduces change, it will always be change of an existing course

---

[2] Dewey's approach is sometimes characterized as instrumentalism, also by Dewey himself. Whereas instrumentalism is generally taken as the view that *theories* are instruments or tools, Dewey's instrumentalism is about the instrumental character of objects of knowledge.

of events. We cannot create out of nothing. For Dewey the only possible construction is a *reconstruction*.

Consequences of pragmatism

One of the most important implications of Dewey's transactional approach is that knowledge does *not* provide us with a picture of reality as it is in itself – an idea to which Dewey referred as the 'spectator theory of knowledge'. For Dewey knowledge always concerns the *relationship* between (our) actions and (their) consequences. This, in essence, is what a transactional conception of knowledge implies. It means that knowledge is a construction, or, to be more precise, that the objects of knowledge are constructions. But contrary to how constructivism is often understood under the mind-world scheme (viz., as purely mental and hence subjective), Dewey's constructivism is a *transactional* constructivism, a constructivism which holds that knowledge is at the very same time constructed *and* real. This is why we can call Dewey's position a form of realism, albeit *transactional realism* (Sleeper 1986).

Given that knowledge concerns the relationship between (our) actions and (their) consequences, knowledge will only ever offer us *possibilities* but not certainty. The conclusions we draw on the basis of careful observation of what follows from how we act upon the world show what has been possible in this particular transactional situation. Sometimes what was possible in one situation turns out also to be possible in another situation, but in other situations, the transactional determinants of the situation are different, so that what was possible in one case is no longer possible in another case (see also chapter 3 on the implications of this idea for the discussion about 'what works'). This is why Dewey preferred to refer to the outcomes of inquiry and research as 'warranted assertions' rather than truth. The assertions we make about the consequences of our actions are warranted on the basis of careful observation and control. But they are only warranted in relation to the particular situation in which they were 'produced', and we shouldn't make the mistake – for example by putting the label 'true' on them – to think that they will be warranted for all time and all similar situations. This does not mean that conclusions from one situation cannot be useful for other situations. But the way in which knowledge from one situation transfers to another situation is, in that it can guide our observation and perception and can suggest possible ways for resolving problems, for finding ways forward. Whether these possibilities will address the specific problems in the specific, new transactional situation can only be discovered when we act.

A more general feature of Dewey's transactional approach to knowing is that, contrary to mainstream modern philosophy, his approach is not a sceptical one. For Dewey there is no gap between human beings and the world. This does not mean that everything we experience is simply 'true'. While Dewey does hold that things are what they are experienced as, there is a crucial difference between experience and knowledge. While experience simply 'is', knowledge, because it has to do with inference, can always be fallible. In this respect we have to conclude that Dewey's transactional theory of knowing is a form of fallibilism. But it is important to see that for Dewey knowledge is *not* fallible because of an alleged gap between ourselves and the world but because we can never be sure what the future will bring, not least because what the future will look like depends also on our own ongoing actions. According to the transactional approach, we are not spectators of a finished universe but participants in an ever-evolving, unfinished universe.

Dewey's transactional approach also cuts across the either/or of objectivism and subjectivism. From a transactional point of view, 'the world' always appears as a function of what we do. Objectivity, understood as a depiction of a world completely independent from and untouched by us, is therefore simply impossible. If we want to know the world, we *must* interact and, as a result, we will only know the world in the way in which it responds to us. The world we construct emerges out of the doing-undergoing-doing dynamics of what Dewey calls 'experience'. One could argue – and many critics of Dewey have done so – that although Dewey rejects objectivism, he thus ends up in a situation of complete subjectivism. Dewey simply acknowledges that this is the case – but he adds that there is no problem with this at all, as long as we see that the worlds we construct are constructed for our own individual purposes, for our own attempts to address the problems we are faced with.

It is only when we start to interact with others that the need for some form of coordination of our subjective worlds with the subjective worlds of others arises. What happens in this case is that, through interaction, cooperation, coordination and communication, we construct an *intersubjective* world out of our individual, subjective worlds. By showing that objectivity is simply not possible, that subjectivity is not always a problem and that intersubjectivity addresses those instances where the subjectivity of knowledge does become a problem, Dewey not only presents us with a position that helps us to overcome the stalemate between objectivism and subjectivism but also hints at a way in which we can overcome the Cartesian Anxiety by showing that we do not have to give up the world when we want to acknowledge that knowledge is always plural, changing and open, and that knowing, most importantly, is always a thoroughly *human* endeavour.

Conclusion: Beyond objectivism and relativism

One thing that is attractive about Dewey's views is that they can make sense of many of the intuitions we hold about knowledge and the world. Rather than creating an opposition between what philosophy tells us and what we seem to be experiencing in our everyday lives, Dewey's ideas are able to capture many of these experiences. Dewey is able to account for the possibility of making a distinction between truth and falsehood; he helps us to see that realism is a reasonable assumption; he can account for the openness of interpretation while at the same time acknowledging that not anything goes, and his transactional approach can also make sense of the advances in technology (see also Hickman 1990). Perhaps Dewey even opens up some possibilities for the idea that we can sometimes indeed speak truth to power.

What is different and distinctive about Dewey's approach is that he does not start from the assumption of the dualism of mind and world but urges us to start from somewhere else and, in doing so, urges us to question and overcome the founding assumptions of modern philosophy rather than positioning ourselves within this framework. In this regard Dewey does indeed manage to go *beyond* objectivism and relativism, to use the title of Richard Bernstein's 1983 book (Bernstein 1983) – and the word 'beyond' is of course of tremendous significance here.

This, as I have tried to make clear, has a number of important implications for the discussion about knowledge, experience and reality. It means the end of the idea of knowledge as a picture of reality and instead puts forward the suggestion that our knowledge is always about *relationships* between actions and consequences. While this does mean that knowledge is a construction, it is not a construction happening somewhere in our head but is a construction 'in transaction', which means that knowledge is both constructed *and* real, that is, linked to our transactions with the world. From this angle the question of truth ceases to be a spatial matter – that is, of the relationship between statements about the world and the world itself – and instead becomes thoroughly temporal – that is, concerned with the relationship between actions and their consequences. Knowledge thus moves from the domain of certainty, the domain of 'what is' to the domain of *possibility*, the domain of 'what might be the case'.

While this opens up new, and in my opinion exciting, opportunities for engaging with questions of knowledge in research and other domains, there is one more technical point that I briefly wish to mention (for more on this see Biesta 2009a, 2011), which has to do with the status of Dewey's contributions to the discussion about knowledge. The issue here is that while, on the one hand, Dewey gives us an account of knowledge as thoroughly practical, connected to our transactions with the world, and therefore located in the domain of the possible not the domain of what is certain, one could argue that in this very account of what knowledge 'is,' Dewey seems to be undermining his own agenda. To put it differently, in his theory of knowledge he seems to fall back on the very position he has been criticizing because he is presenting us with the final truth about what knowledge really is, what the relationship between our knowledge and the world really is, what the place of human beings in the universe is, and so on. One could indeed read Dewey's contribution in this way and then quickly end up in complex but, in a sense, also rather artificial philosophical discussions. The best way forward here, so I wish to suggest, is the pragmatic one, that is, focusing on the question what the *problem* was that Dewey sought to address with his reflections on knowledge. I will outline this briefly here, and will return to it in a bit more detailed way in the next chapter.

The problem that lies behind many if not all of Dewey's writings was what he referred to as the (problematic) impact of modern science on the everyday world, the world of 'common sense', as he put it (see Dewey 1939). While Dewey was happy to acknowledge the advances of modern science and technology, he was concerned about the way in which the scientific world view was colonizing alternative understandings and, more specifically, alternative rationalities. Dewey was concerned, in other words, about the way in which the world view of modern science had become hegemonic, not only in terms of what we hold to be true but also in terms of what we hold to be rational.

Dewey's project, so we might say, was aimed at overcoming the hegemony of modern science, not in an attempt to deny its achievements but in order to reject the idea that it is only science that provides us with access to reality as it really is and that it therefore is only science that can provide us with a standard of what is reasonable or rational.

For Dewey the nub of the problem had to do with the fact that modern science had been interpreted through philosophical categories that *predated* modern science, such as the idea of knowledge as only having to do with what is permanent and fixed – Aristotle's category of the 'eternal' – and of truth as the representation of such a reality 'out there' – Aristotle's category of 'episteme'. Dewey's project, in a sense, was to explore what would happen if, rather than to interpret modern science through pre-scientific philosophical categories, we would interpret science and its claims to knowledge on its own terms. And the outcome of that exercise, as we have seen, is precisely that science can no longer claim to be the possessor of ultimate truth and ultimate rationality. While, at a superficial level, Dewey's work might seem to be singing the praises of modern science, it actually amounts to one of the most fundamental and strategically effective criticisms of the impact of the scientific world view on modern society. It is important to bear this in mind in order not to assume that Dewey is just trying to present us with another 'philosophy to end all philosophies'.

Five questions for discussion and further consideration

1. Is there a (an implicit or explicit) definition of knowledge that informs your research? How would you describe it?
2. Dewey suggests that knowledge is about relationships between actions and consequences. Can you 'read' your own research in this way?
3. According to Dewey, the fact that knowledge is constructed does not mean that it is not 'connected' to reality. Can you make sense of this in relation to your own research?
4. Dewey moves the question of knowledge from the domain of certainty to the domain of possibility. What would that mean for your own research?
5. If knowledge is about *possible* connections between actions and consequences, what would that mean for communicating your research 'findings'?

8

The Political Economy of Academic Publishing

It seems fitting to conclude a book an educational research with a chapter on academic publishing. In the normal – or if one wishes, orthodox – course of events one first conducts the research, and once there are findings and conclusions one publishes results in an appropriate outlet in order to share them with an interested audience, be it with fellow researchers or with other interested parties more widely including, in the case of educational research, educational policy makers and practitioners. Looking at publishing in this way, one might just be grateful that there are publishers who are willing to publish one's work, either in academic journals or as books or book chapters. Such a view forgets, however, that academic publishing has become big business. This is not just in terms of the money that goes around and the profits that are made, quite often from the work that academics do for free, at least from the perspective of academic publishers. It is also because academic journals and, to a lesser extent, academic books have become powerful 'actors' themselves, with academics competing for getting their work published in 'high status' journals, often forgetting or not being aware that what makes a journal into a 'high status' journal is itself big business. This chapter sheds some light on these aspects of academic publishing in order to argue that journals and books are not neutral conduits but are themselves an important part of the research enterprise.

Introduction: The sorcerer's apprentice syndrome

Over the past decade academic publishing has become big business.[1] In a relatively early study on the topic, Cope and Kalantzis (2009), bringing together

---

[1] In this chapter I will mainly use the word 'academic' rather than 'scientist' and 'scientific', partly in order to be able to include the widest possible spectrum of scholarly work and partly in order not to use a word that often comes with particular (positive or negative) connotations. The word

information from a number of publications, provide the following revealing summary of what is going on in what they term 'the knowledge business'.

'In 2004 ... academic publishing in the Western world was dominated by twelve publishing corporations with combined annual sales of approximately $65 billion and employing in the order of 250,000 employees' (Peters, 2009). 'In 2006 the top ten STM [Scientific, Technical and Medical] publishers took in 53% of the revenue in the $16.1 billion [U.S.] periodicals market' (Shreeves, 2009). Universities spend between 0.5 percent and 1.00 percent of their budgets on journals subscriptions (Phillips, 2009). Morgan Stanley reports that academic journals have been the fastest growing media sub-sector of the past 15 years (Morgan Stanley, 2002). An analysis of Ulrich's periodicals list shows that the number of scholarly journals increased from 39,565 in 2003 to 61,620 in 2008; of these, the number of refereed journals has risen from 17,649 in 2002 to 23,973 in 2008. The number of articles per journal is up from 72 per annum in 1972 to 123 in 1995 and average length of an article increased by 80 percent between 1975 and 2007 (Tenopir and King, 2009). Approximately 5.7 million people work in research and development worldwide, publishing on average one article per year, and reading 97 articles per year. This average publication rate per R&D worker per annum has stayed steady, and the dramatic increase in articles published in recent decades is attributable to increases in the number of R&D workers (Mabe and Amin, 2002), (Cope and Kalantizis, 2009).

The amount of money that is involved in publisher take-over deals not only shows how big the financial stakes in academic publishing are but also gives a strong indication of the profitability of the sector. For example, the British private equity group Candover and Cinven created Springer Science and Business Media in 2003 through the acquisition of Kluwer Academic Publishers for €600m and Bertelsmann Springer for €1bn. They subsequently sold the company in 2009 to EQT, a Swedish private equity group, and Singapore's sovereign wealth fund GIC for €2.3bn, making a profit of €700m in as little as six years.[2] While one could argue that academic publishers provide

'academic' is first of all meant as a social category, that is, denoting (the work of) those based in the academia (which, of course, raises further questions about what constitutes the identity and the borders of the academia).

[2] http://www.telegraph.co.uk/finance/newsbysector/banksandfinance/6790251/Candover-and-Cinven-sell-Springer-Science-and-Business-Media-to-EQT-and-GIC-in-2bn-deal.html accessed 28 February 2019.

an important service, both to the academic community and to the public at large, that is, both to 'producers' and 'users' of knowledge – and this is indeed what they do as well – this service comes at a high cost, particularly when one considers that the profit is made from academic work which, to a large extent, is funded by public monies.

If this was all that was happening in the knowledge business, then perhaps the only critical question to ask would be about the size of the profit levels. But academics not only tend to offer their publicly paid work largely for free to commercial publishers but also subsequently need to pay for accessing this work, either through journal subscription fees or increasingly through publication fees (called 'open access fees' or 'manuscript processing fees'). Academic publishers thus act as a 'middle man' between the producers and the consumers of academic writing but, unlike what is the case in most other spheres of economic activity in which 'middle men' operate, in the case of academic publishing producers and consumers are to a large extent part of one and the same community (see McGuigan & Russell 2008; see also The Wellcome Trust 2003).

While one could still argue that this is perhaps the price to pay for an efficient infrastructure which not only facilitates communication among academics across the globe but also plays an important role in safeguarding the quality of academic publication through supporting a system of peer review – which would, of course, be a very charitable interpretation of the situation – this very infrastructure is also increasingly being used to create distinctions *within* the field of academic publishing. Currently the main player here is Thomson Reuters which, with its 'Web of Science' and 'Web of Knowledge' and devices such as the Social Science Citation Index, is having a significant impact on the dynamics of academic publishing and, through this, on the dynamics of academic work itself (see, for example, Craig & Ferguson 2009).

Many countries have seen the introduction of systems where academics are either encouraged or even obliged to publish in journals listed in such indexes, and in some cases only publications in journals with a Thompson Reuters impact factor of at least a certain value 'count'. Not only are individual academic careers increasingly dependent on such systems, for example when decisions on promotion, tenure or research funding are based on the number of publications in particular journals or particular kinds of journals, but the financing of higher education itself is increasingly being made dependent upon this, for example in cases where public funding for research is directly linked to the number of publications generated by a research unit or university as a whole in journals of a particular kind.[3]

One can see, therefore, that what started out as an infrastructure for *supporting* academic activity is increasingly *imposing* its own 'system logic' on this work, thus creating perverse incentives that run the risk of distorting the very point and purpose of academic activity.[4] We can see these developments as an example of what Habermas (1985) has referred to as the colonization of lifeworlds by the 'rationality' of the very systems that were set up to alleviate these lifeworlds from the burden of performing certain tasks. With a more vivid image, I suggest calling it the 'Sorcerer's Apprentice Syndrome', as what we are seeing is that a system that was developed in order to *assist* academic activity has run out of (our) control and is increasingly shaping and controlling the activity itself. One point where the contradictions of the situation become clearly visible is in the fact that whereas the business of academic publishing is clearly geared towards *competition*, it relies at the very same time on traditional academic values of disinterestedness and cooperation in order to sustain itself. After all, without the willingness of academics to provide peer review (and in most cases provide it for free), the whole infrastructure of academic publishing would collapse rapidly.

Setting academic publishing free?

Some people see the interference of corporate business in academic publishing as the main problem and argue that the only way to go is to free academic

---

[3] It is interesting (and worrying) to see that these developments can often be found in smaller countries that wish to emulate the 'success' of academic research in bigger countries without having a real understanding of academic cultures and practices in such countries. Smaller countries such as Norway, Belgium or the Netherlands often take the UK as an example; yet it is interesting that in national research evaluation exercises in the UK (which have been conducted since the early 1990s under the name of Research Assessment Exercise (RAE), which has now been rebranded as Research Excellence Framework), funding decisions are based on peer judgement of the *quality* of academic work and explicitly not its quantity. (In recent rounds RAE panels have based their judgement on four submitted publications per academic published over a period of six to seven years; in the most recent iteration, REF 2021 this has been changed into a minimum of one and maximum of five publications over the evaluation period per individual academic.)

[4] One such distortion has to do with the forms of strategic behaviour that are triggered – or perhaps one can say, rewarded – by these developments. To what extent, after all, can one blame the strategic actions of individual academics if they find themselves in a situation in which their career, the funding for their work and even the financial sustainability of their institutions as a whole become entirely dependent upon the *quantity* of their academic production rather than their *quality*?

publishing from its control. That this line of thinking is gaining momentum can be seen not only from the exponential growth of open access journal publishing but also from a wider discussion among academics and policy makers about the future of academic publishing (see, for example, Willinsky 2006; Peters 2007; OECD 2004; European Commission 2006[5]), and more recently the rise of the idea of 'open science' (see, for example, Nielsen 2011; Albagli, Maciel & Abdo 2015).

While these are significant developments, we should, of course, not be so naive as to assume that to free academic publishing from the control of commercial publishers would move it to an interest-free zone. While the internet has indeed profoundly changed opportunities for communication and dissemination, Microsoft, Google and Facebook – to name just some of the largest profit-makers in the field – are in no way more altruistic than the group of global companies that currently controls the majority of the infrastructure of academic publishing. While the lines of command and control may be different, we should not assume, therefore, that we can simply detach academic publishing from its political economy. That this is so is perhaps most visible in the rapid growth of more or less obscure commercial companies that are setting up open access journals. While such companies often take the moral high ground by emphasizing the virtues of open access publishing, their business model is roughly the same as that of traditional academic publishing in that their ultimate aim is to make a profit and, more interestingly, to do so by trying to get academic labour – and academic credibility – for free.

In finding a way out of the conundrum that contemporary academic publishing appears to be in, it is not only important to be creative, optimistic and imaginative (and here I want to give credit to a variety of open access initiatives, albeit that they are not without problems, as I will indicate below). It is also important, before we start looking for 'answers' or 'solutions', to reflect on the questions we are asking and on the assumptions that come with posing our questions and formulating our problems in a particular way. When the question about the role of academic publishing is phrased in terms of the question who should have control over scientific knowledge production and dissemination, there is first of all the question whether we understand academic

---

[5] See also the UN World Summit on the Information Society: https://www.itu.int/net/wsis/docs/g eneva/official/dop.html (accessed 6 August 2019).

activity well enough if we understand it (entirely) in terms of (the production of) knowledge. In addition there is the question of whose knowledge we are actually talking about and, more specifically, whether it is academics who run the risk of losing control over 'their' knowledge or whether there is the deeper or wider question of whether knowledge can and ought to be possessed by particular individuals and groups in the first place – which is ultimately a political and democratic question.

The epistemic fallacy: Is knowledge the business of 'the knowledge business'?

To think that the essence of academic work is the generation and subsequent dissemination of knowledge – or in more traditional terms, that it is about the disinterested pursuit of truth – is still the much-favoured story that academics tend to tell themselves and others, including their students. Moreover, it is often claimed that academic work produces a particular kind of knowledge, that is, a kind of knowledge that is significantly – and some would even claim, fundamentally – different from everyday knowledge. Here is one version of this story (taken from Cope & Kalantzis 2009):

> Academic or scholarly knowledge has some extraordinary features. It has an intensity of focus and a concentration of intellectual energies greater than that of ordinary, everyday, commonsense or lay knowing. It relies on the ritualistic rigor and accumulated wisdoms of disciplinary communities and their practices. It entails, in short, a kind of systematicity that does not exist in casual experience. Husserl draws the distinction between 'lifeworld' experience and what is 'transcendental' about 'science'. (...) In these terms, the 'lifeworld' is everyday lived experience. The 'transcendental' of academic and scholarly knowledge stands in contradistinction to the commonsense knowing of the lifeworld, which by comparison is relatively unconscious and unreflexive. Academic and scholarly knowledge sets out to comprehend and create meanings-in-the-world which extend more broadly and deeply than the everyday, amorphous pragmatics of the lifeworld. Such knowledge is systematic, premeditated, reflective, purposeful, disciplined and open to scrutiny by a community of experts. Science is more focused and harder work than the knowing in and of the lifeworld.

While in this particular quote the authors do highlight a degree of continuity between everyday knowing and scientific knowing, and in this regard provide a less sharp distinction between the two than what others claim about science – irrespective of the fact that it is actually very difficult if not impossible to find a convincing justification for the idea that science has a distinctive 'essence' (see particularly Woolgar 1988) – they nonetheless seem to take for granted that the 'business' of academic and scholarly work is indeed the generation of knowledge. But when we actually look at what scientists *do*, rather than what we *think* they do, a completely different picture emerges – as has been shown convincingly by many publications from the field of science and technology studies, including Latour's and Woolgar's landmark study *Laboratory Life* (Latour and Woolgar [1979]).

In this book Latour and Woolgar show that scientists – in this particular case those who work at the Salk Institute in California – are involved in a very wide range of different activities, such as the production of written and spoken texts, of techniques and technologies, of practices and protocols, of networks of collaboration and competition and so on. Through these activities, at certain points in time and as a result of very specific processes (which, in *Laboratory Life* Latour and Woolgar characterize as *social* processes although in a later work, particularly in Latour's *Science in Action* from 1987, the analysis is explicitly distinguished from a sociological approach), statements turn into facts and, through a process that Woolgar and Latour call 'splitting and inversion', such facts then become to represent certain objects or phenomena in 'the world'. Or, as they put it in a challenging but precise way, 'The set of statements considered too costly to modify constitute what is referred to as reality' (Latour & Woolgar 1979, p. 243).

To summarize this diversity of activity simply under the heading of 'the generation of knowledge' – often with the assumption that there is a world 'out there' waiting to be discovered, described and explained – not only makes this wide array of activities invisible but also contributes to the creation of a myth about what science and academic work, more generally, actually is. This is not to suggest, of course, that scientific and academic work is fictional – it is far from so – but it is a very different kind of practice generating quite different kind of products and effects than what the story of science as the generation of knowledge seems to suggest.

In this sense the epistemological interpretation of science is a misrepresentation and a mystification and in that regard actually quite unhelpful, both for those at the receiving end of the products of such activities and potentially also for those who do this kind of work, as their self-understanding is often fundamentally epistemological – which also explains why so many students, perhaps more in the social than in the natural sciences, need to sit through long lectures about knowledge, reality and the like. It is not, therefore, that academic work – be it in the sciences, the social sciences or the humanities – doesn't produce anything – it produces things (technology), practices (protocols, ways of acting and doing) and an awful lot of text – but that what it produces is hardly captured adequately with the word 'knowledge'.

Such a different account of what those who call themselves scientists, scholars, researchers or academics do and produce raises two – related – issues for our discussion. On the one hand we can begin to see that the question as to who should be in charge of academic knowledge production and dissemination relies too much on an epistemological interpretation – or as I would prefer to say now, an epistemological *mystification* – of what academic work is 'about'. What the work of such authors as Woolgar and Latour helps us to see is that academic publishing is not something that is 'outside' of the production of scientific facts and of the realities to which such facts correspond – it is not that the 'work' is done first and that, after that, it is reported in academic journals – but that academic publishing is actually an integral part of the process through which certain statements become facts which, in turn, represent certain realities. (I should perhaps emphasize one more time that to talk about facts and realities as social constructions is not meant to make them fictional, even if this is how ideas about social construction are often [mis-] understood by critics.)

The latter insight is particularly prominent in Latour's book *Science in Action* (Latour 1987) where he shows that through the building of longer and stronger networks – networks of quite heterogeneous 'elements', including both things and people – *asymmetries* arise which give strength to some statements, technologies or practices and, in one and the same move, weaken other statements, technologies and practices so that, at some point in time, some of those statements become facts and truths, some of those technologies become inevitable and, at an even more general level, such statements, technologies and practice begin to appear as universal, in that they are everywhere and are able to function everywhere. Again, the point is not to make science or technology fictional. There are technologies that work, and there are statements that make sense. But technologies work under specific conditions and for particular purposes, just as statements make sense in particular contexts and for particular purposes. Yet by connecting them up with a range of other social and material elements, they gain more strength, more status and more presence and begin to become inevitable, so that any attempt to do or say something *different* not only automatically gets labelled as 'alternative' – think about 'alternative' medicine, for example, or 'alternative' schools, for that matter – but is also always in the weaker position so that if an 'alternative' wants to have some influence it needs to invest in lengthening and strengthening its own networks.

On this account – and for further details I refer the reader to Latour's still extremely fascinating book – academic publishing appears as an element in the process of network building, an element that can actually significantly strengthen and lengthen a network. Strength in this regard has a lot to do with the (perceived) status of a journal (and here we can locate the significance of the work of Thompson Reuters is giving some journals more status than others). Length is particularly related to the 'reach' of academic journals, and the more global this reach is the more a journal publication can add to the formation of particular asymmetries. In this way, ideas, insights, technologies and practices that, in themselves, are 'local', so to speak, begin to appear as general, universal and, ultimately, inevitable and thus, in epistemological language, true – simply because it becomes impossible to build a network that is big and strong enough to challenge the other network.

In this regard we can say that Latour does provide us with an understanding of what makes science special. But what is special is not some kind of intrinsic epistemological quality but rather has to do with the strength and length of networks so that what is local begins to appear as general and universal. What Latour particularly highlights is the ability of science to *incorporate* 'society' into its own logic and practice (see particularly Latour 1988), so that modern society should less be understood as the outcome of the application of scientific knowledge on society than as the outcome of the incorporation of a range of local practices and ways of doing and seeing into the logic of science, an incorporation that, interestingly, has been more successful on the 'hard' and 'technological' side of the spectrum – think, for example, of the ways in which the lives of many are at all kind of levels and in all kind of ways incorporated in the logic and practice and medical techno-science – than on the side of the more plural, less technological and in that regard 'softer' social sciences and humanities.

A crisis in rationality

It is one thing to document these processes; yet it is still another to make a judgement about what becomes visible when we look at academic work in this way. One important point here is that the construction of asymmetries not only operates at the level of scientific facts – it is not only about making some statements into facts and other into beliefs. At a deeper or higher level such processes also contribute to a particular articulation of what counts as rational and reasonable; and again, we can see that when a difference becomes staged in terms of regular versus alternative, claims about what is rational and reasonable often play a crucial role. As I already have briefly alluded to in the previous chapter, the whole question of what 'counts' as rational and how some ideas, ways of thinking, ways of doing and ways of seeing become 'counted' as rational, plays an important role in John Dewey's wider intellectual 'project', if, that is, one reads what his work was about carefully.

There is, after all, a rather widespread belief that John Dewey held modern science in high esteem and generally advocated the adoption of the scientific method in all fields of life. Because of this, some have accused Dewey of 'scientism', that is, of the view that what the natural sciences have to say about the world is all there is to say. In his book *Eclipse of Reason* Max Horkheimer argued, for example, that Dewey's 'worship of natural sciences' made it impossible for him to take a critical stance vis-à-vis the sciences and vis-à-vis society more generally (see Horkheimer 1947, pp. 46–9). Whereas Dewey was very clear about the value he attached to the scientific *method* because 'its comparative maturity as a form of knowledge exemplifies so conspicuously the necessary place and function of experimentation' (Dewey 1939, p. 12), he was equally clear that his appreciation for the *methods* of the natural sciences 'would be misinterpreted if it were taken to mean that science is the only valid kind of knowledge' (Dewey 1929, p. 200). Dewey not only rejected the suggestion that the knowledge provided by the natural sciences is the only valid kind of knowledge but also argued against the more general idea that knowledge is the only way in which we can get 'in touch' with reality. If there is one recurring theme in Dewey's work it is precisely his rejection of the idea that knowledge is the 'measure of the reality of [all] other modes of experience' (ibid., p. 235).

According to Dewey the main problem of the identification of what is known with what is real is that it makes it appear as if all other dimensions of human life – such as the practical, aesthetic, ethical or the religious dimensions – can only be real if they can be reduced to and validated by what is revealed through our knowledge. By assuming that knowledge provides the 'norm' for what is real, other aspects of the ways in which human beings live their lives are relegated to the domain of the subjective: the domain of individual taste, points of view, feelings and individual perspectives. As Dewey put it, 'When real objects are identified ... with knowledge-objects, all affectional and volitional objects are inevitably excluded from the "real" world, and are compelled to find refuge in the privacy of an experiencing subject or mind' (Dewey 1925, p. 30). Dewey believed that the identification of what is known with what is real was one of the most fundamental mistakes of modern philosophy and referred to this mistake as the 'intellectualist fallacy' (Dewey 1929, p. 175; see also 1925, pp. 28–30). Yet for Dewey this was not only a *philosophical* problem. It rather was a problem that lay at the heart of modern culture, which was the reason Dewey referred to it as a *crisis* in modern culture (see Dewey 1939). In a sense Dewey's work can be read as a response to this crisis.

According to Dewey the crisis in modern culture is the result of the disintegrating effect of modern science on everyday life. Modern science has completely changed our understanding of the world in which we live. It has given us a view of the world as a mechanism, as 'a scene of indifferent physical particles acting according to mathematical and mechanical laws' (Dewey 1929, p. 33). As a result, modern science 'has stripped the world of the qualities which made it beautiful and congenial to men' (ibid). According to Dewey, the disintegrative impact of this development on the world of everyday life has mainly been caused by the way in which the scientific world view has been *interpreted,* namely as an accurate or 'true' account of reality as it really is. As we have already seen, this has led to the derogation of the reality of the world of everyday experience and of the reality of the non-cognitive dimensions of human lice. As Dewey writes,

> The net practical effect [of this interpretation of the scientific world view] is the creation of the belief that science exists only in the things which are most remote from any significant human concern, so that as we approach social and moral question and interests we must either surrender hope of the guidance of genuine knowledge or else purchase scientific title and authority at the expense of all that is distinctly human. (Dewey 1939, p. 51)

The problem is, in other words, that the realistic interpretation of the mechanistic world view of modern science has put us in a situation in which there are two equally unattractive options: the 'inhuman rationality' of modern science or the 'human *irrationality*' of everyday life. According to Dewey, this predicament lies at the heart of the crisis in culture, which means that this crisis should first and foremost be understood as a crisis of rationality.

The fact that Dewey relates the crisis in culture to a specific *interpretation* of the mechanistic world view of modern science should not be read to imply that the crisis is only a theoretical problem and therefore has nothing to do with the urgent practical problems of contemporary life. Dewey rather wants to stress that the hegemony of scientific rationality and the scientific world view – that is, the situation in which it is assumed that rationality only has to do with the 'hard facts' of science and not with values, morals, feelings, emotions and so on – makes it almost impossible to find an adequate solution for these problems, since the situation we are in is one in which rationality gets restricted to facts and means, while values and ends are, by definition, excluded from rational deliberation. What makes all this even more urgent is the fact that to a large extent modern life is what it is as a result of the 'embodiment of science in the common-sense world', as Dewey puts it (Dewey 1938, p. 81). We are, after all, constantly confronted by the products and effects of modern science, particularly through the omnipresence of technology in our lives, which seems to prove again and again the truth of the scientific world view upon which it is based. This is why Dewey claimed that the world of everyday experience 'is a house divided against itself' (Dewey 1938, p. 84).

Dewey attributes the idea that science provides us with an access to reality as it 'really' is to what he refers to as the spectator theory of knowledge (Dewey 1929, p. 19), a conception of knowledge that goes back to Greek philosophy and the idea of knowledge as a question of vision and of real or true knowledge as having to do with what is fixed and immutable – Aristotle's 'eternal'. Dewey's crucial insight is that when modern experimental science emerged, there were two options. One was to interpret the outcomes of modern experimental science in terms of the Greek spectator theory of knowledge. This was indeed the option taken, so that it was assumed that the insights from the new science presented us with ultimate truths about the world. The option that was not taken was to 'update' our understanding of knowledge in light of the fact that modern experimental science did not generate its outcomes through observation – through what Dewey elsewhere termed a 'Kodak' picture of the world – but through active intervention, a process that, from the perspective of the spectator theory of knowledge, creates problems because it 'troubles' the very object it wishes to depict. It was, however, the second option – that is, of bringing our understanding of knowledge in line with the experimental and interventionist ways of modern science – which Dewey pursued in his own work, leading him to a theory of knowing rather than a theory of knowledge and understanding knowledge in terms of the relationship between actions and consequences, not a picture of a static world 'out there'. This, as I have discussed in the previous chapter, moves knowledge from the plane of certainty to the domain of possibility. And it reveals that so-called 'scientific' knowledge is not knowledge of a particular quality – more true, for example, than everyday knowledge – but knowledge that has been generated through particular ways of doing (experimentation) and in specific social settings (such as universities, laboratories, etc.).

In this way, as mentioned, Dewey provides us with an effective critique of the suggestion that science provides us with a particular 'kind' of knowledge that is more true and more real and should therefore have not only *epistemological* power over us but also – and this is at the heart of what Dewey sees as the crisis in culture – normative power, that is, that we should adjust ourselves to such knowledge, rather than that we have control over it. At stake in Dewey's account are therefore ultimately questions of power, that is, whether we let 'scientific' knowledge have power over us or whether we reclaim and regain power over scientific knowledge and see it for what it is: potentially useful in particular situations but not more powerful or more rational than what emerges in other domains of human life.

Conclusions

From the rather concrete questions about the role and impact of the global publishing industry on academic publishing with which I have started this chapter, we have ended up with a much larger issue that has to do with the question in what ways and to what extent our research is contributing to the creation of asymmetries – for example between scientific and everyday knowledge, or between those who 'know' and those who merely have 'opinions' – or whether it is playing a role in interrupting and questioning such asymmetries. That is why freeing up academic publishing by taking it out of the hands of the global publishing industry is, in itself, not really a liberation if the alternatives that emerge still are engaged in forms of publishing that contribute to the creation of asymmetries, the creation of differences between longer and shorter and between stronger and weaker networks. While the issue of academic publishing is not insignificant in all this, as I have tried to show, the much 'bigger' question it raises is the extent to which 'we' as academics, scholars, social and educational scientists are involved in the reduction of options for thinking and doing, or whether we are motivated by attempts to pluralize thinking and doing so as to contribute to the democratization of knowledge production and dissemination, an issue that is particularly relevant for research that seeks to make education better and enhance the scope for professional action.

What might be done to move in that direction? One important step is that we start providing our students, as well as ourselves, with different accounts of what it means to be a (an academic) researcher – not accounts focused on epistemology and ontology but rather accounts focused on politics and democracy and on the public responsibility of academic researchers. Similarly, we should improve the accounts we give about what it is that we are actually doing when we are involved in the conduct of research, and we should educate policy makers, politicians, practitioners and the wider public about the possibilities and limitations of what research can offer, particularly addressing misunderstanding about the alleged special nature of scientific research – which we can begin to do by highlighting that 'scientific' is not an epistemological category but a thoroughly *social* one. The critical question in all this is whether we aim to contribute to strengthening and lengthening of networks so that opportunities for different forms of acting and being become reduced, or whether we position our work in opposition to this, so that we contribute to a democratic pluralization of opportunities for action and being – and the word 'democratic' is of course crucial here, so that we do not forget that not every pluralization, not every 'opening up', automatically leads to the realization of democratic freedom and equality.

Might academic publishing be able to play a role in all this? I think it can, if we approach the question of publishing itself in a way that is political and responsible. But this is a huge challenge in many countries, perhaps not even so much because of the particular role of the global publishing industry, but far more because of the ways in which some use this machinery to control the work of academics.

Five questions for discussion and further consideration

1. What role does publishing play in your research? Are you obliged to publish? Are you allowed to publish? Who decides?
2. Do you think that researchers should pay for getting their work published? Why? Why not?
3. Will your research strengthen or weaken particular asymmetries? Which ones? How?
4. How do you see the relationship between findings or insights from your researchers and the views educational practitioners have?
5. What are your views on the relationships between academic research and democracy?

Epilogue: Too Much Research?

In Chapter 1 I posed 'the most difficult question', which was the question why we actually should be doing research at all. This is not the most difficult question in a general sense, but it is a pretty difficult question for researchers, as an honest answer to the question could mean that one would stop doing research or not even embark on it. Posing the question is important, in my view, because we cannot and shouldn't assume that for every problem we encounter, in education or elsewhere, research is the most appropriate way for addressing or solving it. Rather than assuming that research starts with the formulation of research questions – one of the orthodoxies one may find in introductions to educational research – it makes more sense to start with an identification of the problem in order then to ask whether research is the most appropriate way for addressing the problem. Sometimes the answer to that question will be 'yes', in which case it is justified to begin developing an appropriate research design, but sometimes the answer will be 'no', in which case researchers should withdraw.

While this sounds easy, it may actually be quite difficult to do. One reason for this has to do with the fact that we live in a time where there is (still, one might say) a strong belief in the positive power of research. Research, particularly if it is preceded by the word 'scientific', is often still perceived as a superior kind of knowledge with cognitive *and* normative power, a kind of knowledge that therefore should overrule everyday knowledge. While one may expect that researchers conduct their work in careful, thoughtful and transparent ways – although we also know that this is not always the case – it is an illusion to assume that this generates knowledge that is *structurally* different from everyday knowledge. It is at most *gradually* different and should therefore always be taken with caution. This is not, as I have said before, in order to denigrate research, but to make it not bigger or more important than it is, even if the expectation from 'outside' is different – which can be quite a seductive expectation for researchers.

A second reason why it may be difficult to confess that in some situations research has nothing to offer, has to do with the sheer size of the contemporary research 'enterprise'. There are many universities around the world with many academics working in them, and whereas in the past it may have been enough for a substantial number of them to engage with teaching and their own scholarship, there is a still increasing pressure on everyone to produce – the phrase 'publish or perish' still describes the job situation of many academics quite accurately – which, ironically, creates a 'need' for research; that is, that many academics who find themselves under pressure to publish are in need of things they can do research on. This is perhaps even a bigger problem for the field of educational research, particularly in those countries where teacher education is or has become part of universities, thus significantly expanding the 'labour force' in academic departments of education. There is, therefore, perhaps more supply of then demand for research, which is another reason why it might be difficult to answer 'the most difficult question' in an honest way.

In addition to a potential overcapacity of academic researchers, there is a further development in the field of education that could exacerbate the problem, which is not so much the push to turn teaching into an evidence-based profession – which tends to position teachers as users of research – but the increasing trend for teachers to become researchers of their own practice. One strand of this development is actually quite old and has its roots in educational action research – a mode of research in the practice of education, by practitioners, aimed at addressing 'local' problems in a systematic way. Although even here one needs to be mindful that research is only one way to engage with one's practice and only one way to address the problems one may encounter there, the methods utilized in action research were, and still are, generally appropriate for the specific character of the practice of education. More recently, however, methods that stem from effectiveness research, particularly the randomized controlled trial, are beginning to be used by teachers in order to find out which particular 'intervention' is most 'effective'. While it may sound tempting to think of one's teaching as an intervention and see student learning – or their test scores – as the effect of such interventions, the suggestion that the 'logic' of research and the 'logic' of teaching are roughly the same is actually quite problematic.

One important difference between teaching and research is that the purpose of research, with all the provisos presented in the preceding chapters, is to generate knowledge, whereas the purpose of teaching is to educate students. Moreover, as soon as one begins to redefine teaching as an intervention that is supposed to bring about certain effects on the side of students, one forgets first and foremost that students are not objects upon which one can intervene – successfully, effectively or otherwise – but that they are subjects: acting, thinking and judging beings. More importantly, the very point of education is to enhance the capacity of students to act, think and judge; the very point of education, to put it differently, is to make sure that at some point students no longer need education but can live their own life, and live it well. This is where the intervention-effect logic that is creeping into the classroom under the name of teacher research is actually producing a distortion of what education is, and this is perhaps the most important reason why we shouldn't conflate teaching and research and should not assume that when teachers become researchers of their own practice, they will automatically become better teachers.

Is this, ultimately, then an argument *against* educational research? That would be a misreading of what I have tried to do in this book. My ambition has rather been to show with more precision what research is and what it is not; what we can legitimately expect from research and where there are limits; how it can help the improvement of education and where it begins to hinder such an ambition; and also, therefore, that research is not necessarily or automatically beneficial for the practice of education. My hope is that this may help beginning researchers in gaining a perspective *on* the orthodoxies of educational research rather than simply accepting or having to accept them as the right and one-and-only way to understand and do research, in, on and for education.

References

Achinstein, P. & Barker, S.F. (1969). *The legacy of logical positivism: Studies in the philosophy of science*. Baltimore, MD: Johns Hopkins Press.

Albagli, S., Maciel, M.L. & Abdo, A.H. (Eds.) (2015). *Open science, open issues*. Brasília: IBICT; Rio de Janeiro: Unirio.

Alexander, R. (2004). Still no pedagogy? Principle, pragmatism and compliance in primary education. *Cambridge Journal of Education 24*(1), 7–34.

Aristotle (1980). *The Nichomachean ethics*. Translated with an introduction by David Ross. Oxford/New York: Oxford University Press.

Ax, J. & Ponte, P. (2010). Moral issues in educational praxis: A perspective from *pedagogiek* and *didactiek* as human sciences in continental Europe. *Pedagogy, Culture & Society 18*(1), 29–42.

Ayer, A.J. (1959). *Logical positivism*. Glencoe, IL: Free Press.

Bachelard, G. (1986[1949]). *Le rationalisme appliqué*. Paris: Presses Universitaires de France.

Ball, S. (2003). The teacher's soul and the terror of performativity. *Journal of Education Policy 18*(2), 215–28.

Benner, D. (2005). *Allgemeine Pädagogik*, 5th edition. Weinheim/München: Juventa.

Bernstein, R.J. (1983). *Beyond objectivism and relativism: Science, hermeneutics, and praxis*. Philadelphia: University of Pennsylvania Press.

Biesta, G.J.J. (2005). What can critical pedagogy learn from postmodernism? Further reflections on the impossible future of critical pedagogy. In I. Gur Ze'ev (Ed.), *Critical theory and critical pedagogy today: Toward a new critical language in education* (pp. 143–59). Haifa: University of Haifa Studies in Education.

Biesta, G.J.J. (2006). *Beyond learning: Democratic education for a human future*. Boulder, CO: Paradigm Publishers.

Biesta, G.J.J. (2007). Why 'what works' won't work: Evidence-based practice and the democratic deficit of educational research. *Educational Theory 57*(1), 1–22.

Biesta, G.J.J. (2009a). How to use pragmatism pragmatically: Suggestions for the 21st century. In A.G. Rud, J. Garrison & L. Stone (Eds.), *John Dewey at 150: Reflections for a new century* (pp. 30–9). Lafayette, IN: Purdue University Press.

Biesta, G.J.J. (2009b). Values and ideals in teachers' professional judgement. In S. Gewirtz, P. Mahony, I. Hextall & A. Cribb (Eds.), *Changing teacher professionalism* (pp. 184–93). London: Routledge.

Biesta, G.J.J. (2009c). Good education in an age of measurement: On the need to reconnect with the question of purpose in education. *Educational Assessment, Evaluation and Accountability 21*(1), 33–46.

Biesta, G.J.J. (2010a). A new 'logic' of emancipation: The methodology of Jacques Rancière. *Educational Theory 60*(1), 39–59.

Biesta, G.J.J. (2010b). Pragmatism and the philosophical foundations of mixed methods research. In A. Tashakkori & C. Teddlie (Eds.), Sage *handbook of mixed methods in social and behavioral research*, 2nd edition (pp. 95–118). Thousand Oaks, CA: Sage.

Biesta, G.J.J. (2010c). Five these on complexity reduction and its politics. In D.C. Osberg & G.J.J. Biesta (Eds.), *Complexity theory and the politics of education* (pp. 5–14). Rotterdam: Sense Publishers.

Biesta, G.J.J. (2010d). Why 'what works' still won't work: From evidence-based education to value-based education. *Studies in Philosophy and Education 29*(5), 491–503.

Biesta, G.J.J. (2010e). Learner, student, speaker: Why it matters how we call those we teach. *Educational Philosophy and Theory 42*(4), 540–52.

Biesta, G.J.J. (2010f). *Good Education in an age of measurement: Ethics, politics, democracy*. Boulder, CO: Paradigm Publishers.

Biesta, G.J.J. (2010g). An alternative future for European educational research. *Zeitschrift für Pädagogische Historiographie 16*(1), 105–7.

Biesta, G.J.J. (2011). Welches Wissen ist am meisten wert? Zur Veränderung des öffentlichen Status von Wissenschaft und Wissen im Feld der Erziehung. In A. Schäfer & C. Thompson (Eds.), *Wissen* (pp. 77–97). Paderborn: Schöningh Verlag.

Biesta, G.J.J. (2012). Giving teaching back to education. *Phenomenology and Practice 6*(2), 35–49.

Biesta, G.J.J. (2013a). Learning in public places: Civic learning for the 21st century. In G.J.J. Biesta, M. de Bie & D. Wildemeersch (Eds.), *Civic learning, democratic citizenship and the public sphere* (pp. 1–11). Dordrecht/Boston: Springer.

Biesta, G.J.J. (2013b). Interrupting the politics of learning. *Power and Education 5*(1), 4–15.

Biesta, G.J.J. (2017a). Don't be fooled by ignorant schoolmasters: On the role of the teacher in emancipatory education. *Policy Futures in Education 15*(1), 52–73.

Biesta, G.J.J. (2017b). *The rediscovery of teaching*. London/New York: Routledge.

Biesta, G.J.J., Allan, J. & Edwards, R.G. (2011). The theory question in research capacity building in education: Towards an agenda for research and practice. *British Journal of Educational Studies 59*(3), 225–39.

Biesta, G.J.J. & Burbules, N. (2003). *Pragmatism and educational research*. Lanham, MD: Rowman and Littlefield.

Biesta, G.J.J., Field, J., Hodkinson, P., Macleod, F.J. & Goodson, I.F. (2011). *Improving learning through the lifecourse: Learning lives*. London/New York: Routledge.

Bingham, C. (2008). *Authority is relational*. Albany, NY: SUNY Press.

Björkman, J.W. (1982). Professionalism in the welfare state: Sociological saviour or political pariah? *European Journal of Political Research 10*(4), 407–28.

Bloor, D. (1983). *Wittgenstein: A social theory of meaning*. London/New York: MacMillan.

Bogotch, I., Mirón, L. & Biesta, G. (2007). 'Effective for what; Effective for whom?' Two questions SESI should not ignore. In T. Townsend (Ed.), *International handbook of school effectiveness and school improvement* (pp. 93–110). Dordrecht/ Boston: Springer.

Braunmühl, E. von (1975). *Antipädagogik*. Weinheim: Juventa.

Bridges, D. (2006). The disciplines and discipline of educational research. *Journal of Philosophy of Education 40*(2), 259–72.

Brown, A. (2009). *Higher skills development at work: A commentary by the Teaching and Learning Research Programme*. London: ESRC/TLRP.

Carr, D. (1992). Practical enquiry, values and the problem of educational theory. *Oxford Review of Education 18* (3), 241–51.

Carr, W. (2006). Education without theory. *British Journal of Educational Studies 54*(2), 136–59.

Carr, W. & Kemmis, S. (1986). *Becoming critical*. London: Routledge.

Charlton, B.G. (2002). Audit, accountability, quality and all that: The growth of managerial technologies in UK Universities. In S. Prickett & P. Erskine-Hill (Eds.), *Education! Education! Education! Managerial ethics and the law of unintended consequences* (pp. 13–28). Exeter: Imprint Academic.

Cope, W. & Kalantzis, M. (2009). Signs of epistemic disruption: Transformations in the knowledge system of the academic journal. *First Monday 14*(4). Available online at: http://firstmonday.org/htbin/cgiwrap/bin/ojs/index.php/fm/rt/printer Friendly/2309/2163.

Cornish, F. & Gillespie, A. (2009). A pragmatist approach to the problem of knowledge in health psychology. *Journal of Health Psychology 14*(6), 800–9.

Coulter, D. & Wiens, J. (2002). Educational judgement: Linking the actor to the spectator. *Educational Research 31*(4), 15–25.

Craig, I. D. & Ferguson, L. (2009). Journals ranking and impact factors: How the performance of journals is measured. In B. Cope & A. Phillips (Eds.), *The future of the academic journal* (pp. 159–94). Oxford: Chandos.

Dancy, J. (1985). *An introduction of contemporary epistemology*. Oxford: Basil Blackwell.

David, M. et al. (n.d.). *Effective learning and teaching in UK Higher Education: A commentary by the Teaching and Learning Research Programme*. London: ESRC/ TLRP.

Dewey, J. (1896). The reflex arc concept in psychology. In Jo Ann Boydston (Ed.), *John Dewey: The early works (1882–1898)*, Volume 5 (pp. 224–43). Carbondale and Edwardsville: Southern Illinois University Press.

Dewey, J. (1905). The postulate of immediate empiricism. In Jo Ann Boydston (Ed.), *John Dewey: The middle works (1899–1924)*, Volume 3 (pp. 158–67). Carbondale and Edwardsville: Southern Illinois University Press.

Dewey, J. (1906). The experimental theory of knowledge. In Jo Ann Boydston (Ed.), *John Dewey: The middle works (1899–1924)*, Volume 3 (pp. 107–27). Carbondale and Edwardsville: Southern Illinois University Press.

Dewey, J. (1907). The control of ideas by facts. In Jo Ann Boydston (Ed.), *John Dewey: The middle works (1899–1924)*, Volume 4 (pp. 78–90). Carbondale and Edwardsville: Southern Illinois University Press.

Dewey, J. (1911). Epistemology. In Jo Ann Boydston (Ed.), *John Dewey: The middle works (1899–1924)*, Volume 6 (pp. 440–2). Carbondale and Edwardsville: Southern Illinois University Press.

Dewey, J. (1916). Introduction to *Essays in experimental logic*. In Jo Ann Boydston (Ed.), *John Dewey: The middle works (1899–1924)*, Volume 10 (pp. 320–69). Carbondale and Edwardsville: Southern Illinois University Press.

Dewey, J. (1920). *Reconstruction in philosophy*. In Jo Ann Boydston (Ed.), *John Dewey: The middle works (1899–1924)*, Volume 12 (pp. 77–201). Carbondale and Edwardsville: Southern Illinois University Press.

Dewey, J. (1922). *Human nature and conduct*. In Jo Ann Boydston (Ed.), *John Dewey: The middle works (1899–1924)*, Volume 14. Carbondale and Edwardsville: Southern Illinois University Press.

Dewey, J. (1925). *Experience and nature*. In Jo Ann Boydston (Ed.), *John Dewey: The later works (1925–1953)*, Volume 1. Carbondale and Edwardsville: Southern Illinois University Press.

Dewey, J. (1929). *The quest for certainty*. In Jo Ann Boydston (Ed.), *John Dewey: The later works (1925–1953)*, Volume 4. Carbondale and Edwardsville: Southern Illinois University Press.

Dewey, J. (1933). How we think: A restatement of the relation of reflective thinking to the educative process. In Jo Ann Boydston (Ed.), *John Dewey: The later works (1925–1953)*, Volume 8 (pp. 105–352). Carbondale and Edwardsville: Southern Illinois University Press.

Dewey, J. (1938). Logic: The theory of inquiry. In Jo Ann Boydston (Ed.), *John Dewey: The later works (1925–1953)*, Volume 12. Carbondale and Edwardsville: Southern Illinois University Press.

Dewey, J. (1939). Experience, knowledge and value: A rejoinder. In Jo Ann Boydston (Ed.), *John Dewey: The later works (1925–1953)*, Volume 14 (pp. 3–90). Carbondale and Edwardsville: Southern Illinois University Press.

Dewey, J. (1966[1916]). *Democracy and education*. New York: The Free Press.

Dunne, J. (1992). *Back to the rough ground*. Notre Dame, IN: University of Notre Dame Press.

Eagleton, T. (2007). *Ideology: An introduction*, New and updated edition. London/New York: Verso.

European Commission. (2006). *Study on the economic and technical evolution of scientific publication markets in Europe*. Available online at: http://ec.europa.eu/research/science-society/pdf/scientificpublication-study_en.pdf.

Faulks, K. (1998). *Citizenship in modern Britain*. Edinburgh: Edinburgh University Press.

Feinberg, W. (2001). Choice, autonomy, need-definition and educational reform. *Studies in Philosophy and Education 20*(5), 402–9.

Fenstermacher, G. (1986). Philosophy of research on teaching: Three aspects. In M.C. Wittrock (Ed.), *Handbook of research on teaching*, 3rd edition. Washington, DC: AERA.

Foucault, M. (1970). *The order of things: An archaeology of the human sciences*. New York: Pantheon Books.

Freidson, E. (1994). *Professionalism reborn: Theory, prophecy, and policy*. Chicago IL: University of Chicago Press.

Freire, P. (1970). *Pedagogy of the oppressed*. New York: Continuum.

Gettier, E. (1963). Is justified true belief knowledge? *Analysis 23*(6), 121–3.

Gewirtz, S. (2001). *The managerial school: Post-welfarism and social justice in education*. London/New York: Routledge.

Gieryn, T.F. (1983). Boundary-work and the demarcation of science from non-science: Strains and interests in professional ideologies of scientists. *American Sociological Review 48*, 781–95.

Gieryn, T.F. (1999). *Cultural boundaries of science: Credibility on the line*. Chicago, IL: University of Chicago Press.

Goodson, I., Biesta, G.J.J., Tedder, M. & Adair, N. (2010). *Narrative learning*. London/New York: Routledge.

Groothoff, H.-H. (1973). Theorie der Erziehung. In H.-H. Groothoff (Ed.), *Pädagogik Fischer Lexikon* (pp. 72–9). Frankfurt am Main: Fischer Taschenbuch Verlag.

Guba, E.G. & Lincoln, Y.S. (1994). Competing paradigms in qualitative research. In N. Denzin & Y. Lincoln (Eds.), *Handbook of qualitative research* (pp. 105–17). Thousand Oaks, CA: SAGE.

Gundem, B.B. & Hopmann, S. (Eds.) (1998). *Didaktik and/or curriculum. An international dialogue*. New York: Peter Lang.

Guyatt, G., Cairns, J., Churchill, D., et al. (1992). Evidence-based medicine. A new approach to teaching the practice of medicine. *JAMA 268*, 2420–5.

Habermas, J. (1968). *Erkenntnis und Interesse*. Frankfurt am Main: Suhrkamp.

Habermas, J. (1970). *Zur Logik der Sozialwissenschaften.* Frankfurt am Main: Suhrkamp.

Habermas, J. (1971). *Knowledge and human interests.* Boston: Beacon Press.

Habermas, J. (1985). *The theory of communicative action. Volume 1: Reason and the rationalization of society.* Boston, MA: Beacon Press.

Habermas, J. (1990). *On the logic of the social sciences.* Cambridge, MA: MIT Press.

Hammersley, M. (2005). The myth of research-based practice: The critical case of educational inquiry. *International Journal of Social Research Methodology 8*(4), 317–30.

Hammersley, M. (2009). What is evidence for evidence-based practice? In R. St. Clair (Ed.), *Education science: Critical perspectives* (pp. 101–11). Rotterdam: Sense.

Hattie, J. (2008). *Visible learning: A synthesis of over 800 meta-analyses relating to achievement.* London/New York: Routledge.

Hellín, T. (2002). The physician–patient relationship: Recent developments and changes. *Haemophilia 8*, 450–4. doi: 10.1046/j.1365-2516.2002.00636.x

Hickman, L. (1990). *John Dewey's pragmatic technology.* Bloomington, IN: Indiana University Press.

Hilvoorde, I. van. (2002). *Grenswachters van de pedagogiek.* Baarn: HB Uitgevers.

Hirst, P.H. (1966). Educational theory. In J.W. Tibble (Ed.), *The study of education* (pp. 29–58). London: Routledge and Kegan Paul.

Hollis, M. (1994). *The philosophy of social science: An introduction.* Cambridge: Cambridge University Press.

Holmes, D., Murray, S.J., Perron, A. & Rail, G. (2006). Deconstructing the evidence-based discourse in health science: Truth, power and facism. *International Journal of Evidence Based Healthcare 4*(3), 160–86.

Horkheimer, M. (1947). *Eclipse of reason.* New York: Oxford University Press.

James, D. & Biesta, G.J.J. (2007). *Improving learning cultures in further education.* London: Routledge.

James, M. & Pollard, A. (2006). *Improving teaching and learning in schools: A commentary by the Teaching and Learning Research Programme.* London: ESRC/TLRP.

James, M. & Pollard, A. (2012a). TLRP's ten principles for effective pedagogy: Rationale, development, evidence, argument and impact, *Research Papers in Education 26*(3), 275–328.

James, M. & Pollard, A. (2012b) Introduction, *Research Papers in Education 26*(3), 269–73.

James, W. (1899). *Talks to teachers on psychology: And to students on some of life's ideals.* New York, NY: Henry Holt and Company.

Keiner, E. (2002). Education between academic discipline and profession in Germany after World War II. *European Educational Research Journal 11*(1), 83–98.

Kessels, J.P.A.M. & Korthagen, F.A.J. (1996). The relationship between theory and practice: Back to the classics. *Educational Researcher 25*(3), 17–22.

König, E. (1975). *Theorie der Erziehungswissenschaft. Band 1.* München: Wilhelm Fink Verlag.

Kunneman, H. (1996). Normatieve professionaliteit: een appèl. *Sociale Interventie 3*, 107–12.

Laing, R.D. (1960). *The divided self: An existential study in sanity and madness.* Harmondsworth: Penguin.

Laing, R.D. & Esterson, A. (1964). *Sanity, madness and the family.* London: Penguin Books.

Latour, B. (1983). Give me a laboratory and I will raise the world. In K.D. Knorr & M. Mulkay (Eds.), *Science observed* (pp. 141–70). London: Sage.

Latour, B. (1987). *Science in action: How to follow scientists and engineers through society.* Milton Keynes: Open University Press.

Latour, B. (1988). *The pasteurization of France.* Cambridge, MA: Harvard University Press.

Latour, B. (2005). *Reassembling the social: An introduction to actor-network-theory.* Oxford: Oxford University Press.

Latour, B. & Woolgar, S. (1979). *Laboratory life: The social construction of scientific facts.* Beverly Hills, CA: Sage.

Law, J. & J. Hassard (Eds.) (1999). *Actor network theory and after.* Oxford/Keele: Blackwell/The Sociological Review.

Lawn, M. & Furlong, J. (2007). The social organisation of education research in England. *European Educational Research Journal 61*(1), 55–70.

Lawn, M. & Furlong, J. (2009). The disciplines of education in the UK: Between the ghost and the shadow. *Oxford Review of Education 35*(5), 541–52.

Leaton Gray, S. (2007). Teacher as technician: Semi-professionalism after the 1988 Education Reform Act and its effect on conceptions of pupil identity. *Policy Futures in Education 5*(2), 194–203.

Levine, D.N. (2006). *Powers of the mind: The reinvention of liberal learning in America.* Chicago, IL: University of Chicago Press.

Manen, M. van (1977). Linking ways of knowing with ways of being practical. *Curriculum Inquiry 6*(3), 205–28.

McCulloch, G. (2002). Disciplines contributing to education? Educational studies and the disciplines. *British Journal of Educational Studies 50*(1), 100–10.

McGuigan, G.S. & Russell, R.D. (2008). The business of academic publishing: A strategic analysis of the academic journal publishing industry and its impact on the future of scholarly publishing. *Electronic Journal of Academic and Special Librarianship 9*(3). Available online at: http:// southernlibrarianship.icaap.org/con tent/v09n03/mcguigan_g01.html (accessed 30 June 2012).

Meirieu, P. (2008). *Pédagogie: Le devoir de résister*, 2e edition. Issy-les-Moulineaux: ESF.

Mouffe, C. (2000). *The democratic paradox*. London/New York: Verso.

Nielsen, M. (2011). *Reinventing discovery: The new era of networked science*. Princeton, NJ: Princeton University Press.

Noordegraaf, M. (2007). From 'pure' to 'hybrid' professionalism: Present-day professionalism in ambiguous public domains. *Administration & Society 39*(6), 761–85.

Noordegraaf, M. & Abma, T. (2003). Management by measurement? Public management practices amidst ambiguity. *Public Administration 81*(4), 853–71.

Nozick, R. (1981). *Philosophical explanations*. Oxford: Oxford University Press.

O'Connor, D.J. (1957). *An introduction to the philosophy of education*. London: Routledge and Kegan Paul.

OECD. (2004). *Declaration on access to research data from public funding*. 30 January 2004, http://www.oecd.org.

Oelkers, J. (1993). Influence and development: Two basic paradigms of education. *Studies in Philosophy and Education 13*(2), 91–109.

Oelkers, J. (2001). *Einführung in die Theorie der Erziehung*. Weinheim & Basel: Beltz.

O'Neill, O. (2002). *BBC Reith lectures 2002: A question of trust*. Retrieved from http://www.bbc.co.uk/radio4/reith2002.

Otto, H.-U., Polutta, A. & Ziegler, H. (2009). A second generation of evidence-based practice: Reflexive professionalism and causal impact in social work. In H.-. Otto, A. Polutta & H. Ziegler (Eds.), *Evidence-based practice: Modernising the knowledge-base of social work* (pp. 245–52). Opladen: Barbara Budrich.

Peters, M.A. (2007). *Knowledge economy: Development and the future of higher education*. Rotterdam: Sense.

Peters, R.S. (1963). Education as initiation. In P. Gordon (Ed.), *The study of education*, Volume 1 (pp. 273–99). London: Woburn.

Peterson, P. (1979). Direct instruction? Effective for what and for whom? *Educational Leadership 37*(1), 46–8.

Phillips, A. (2009). Business models in journals publishing. In B. Cope & A. Phillips (Eds.), *The future of the academic journal*. Oxford: Chandos.

Pinar, W. (Ed.) (1975). *Curriculum theorizing: The reconceptualists*. Berkeley, CA: McCutchan.

Pinar, W. (1999). Introduction: A farewell and a celebration. In W.F. Pinar (Ed.), *Contemporary curriculum discourses* (pp. xi–xx). New York: Peter Lang.

Pinar, W.F., Reynolds, W.M., Slattery, P. & Taubman, P.M. (1995). *Understanding curriculum*. New York: Peter Lang.

Pollard, A. & Oancea, A. (2010). *Unlocking learning? Towards evidence-informed policy and practice in education*. Report of the UK Strategic Forum for Research in Education, 2008–2010. London: SFRE.

Prenzel, M. (2009). Challenges facing the educational system. In *Vital questions: The contribution of European social science* (pp. 30–3). Strasbourg: European Science Foundation.

Priestley, M. & Biesta, G.J.J. (Eds.) (2013). *Reinventing the curriculum: New trends in curriculum policy and practice*. London: Bloomsbury.

Priestley, M., Biesta, G.J.J. & Robinson, S. (2015). *Teacher agency: An ecological approach*. London: Bloomsbury.

Rasmussen, J. (2010). Increasing complexity by reducing complexity: A Luhmannian approach to learning. In D.C. Osberg & G.J.J. Biesta (Eds.), *Complexity theory and the politics of education* (pp. 15–24). Rotterdam: Sense Publishers.

Reid, W.A. (1999). *Curriculum as institution and practice: Essays in the deliberative tradition*. Mahwah, NJ and London: Lawrence Erlbaum.

Rorty, R. (1979). *Philosophy and the mirror of nature*. Princeton, NJ: Princeton University Press.

Schwab, J. (2004). The practical: A language for curriculum. In D.J. Flinders & S.J. Thornton (Eds.), *The curriculum studies reader*, 2nd edition (pp. 103–17). New York: Routledge.

Schwab, J.J. (1969). The practical: A language for curriculum. *The School Review* 78(1), 1–23.

Schwab, J.J. (1971). The practical: Arts of eclectic. *The School Review* 79(4), 493–542.

Schwab, J.J. (1973). The practical 3: Translation into curriculum. *The School Review* 81(4), 501–22.

Schwab, J.J. (1983). The practical 4: Something for curriculum professors to do. *Curriculum Inquiry* 13(3), 239–65.

Shreeves, S.L. (2009). Cannot predict now: The role of repositories in the future of the journal. In B. Cope & A. Phillips (Eds.), *The future of the academic journal* (pp. 197–212). Oxford: Chandos.

Simon, B. (1981). Why no pedagogy in England? In B. Simon & W. Taylor (Eds.), *Education in the eighties: The central issues*. London: Batsford.

Slavin, R. (2002). Evidence-based educational policies: Transforming educational practice and research. *Educational Researcher* 31(7), 15–21.

Sleeper, R.W. (1986). *The necessity of pragmatism: John Dewey's conception of philosophy*. New Haven, CT: Yale University Press.

Smeyers, P. & Depaepe, M. (Eds.) (2006). *Educational research: Why 'what works' doesn't work*. Dordrecht: Springer.

Smith, R. (2006). Technical difficulties: The workings of practical judgement. In
P. Smeyers & M. Depaepe (Eds.), *Educational research: Why 'what works' doesn't
work* (pp. 159–70). Dordrecht: Springer.

St. Clair, R. (Ed.) (2009). *Education science: Critical perspectives*. Rotterdam: Sense.

Stanley, Morgan (2002). *Scientific publishing: Knowledge is power*. London: Morgan
Stanley Equity Research Europe. Available online at: http://www.econ.ucsb.edu/
~tedb/Journals/morganstanley.pdf (accessed 16 March 2009).

Stenhouse, L. (1975). *An introduction to curriculum research and development*.
London: Heinemann.

Tashakkori, A. & Teddlie, C. (Eds.) (2010). *Sage handbook of mixed methods in social
and behavioral research*, 2nd edition. Thousand Oaks, CA: Sage.

Thomas, G. & Pring, R. (Eds.) (2004). *Evidence-based practice in education*. Milton
Keynes: Open University Press.

Tibble, J.W. (Ed.) (1966a). *The study of education*. London: Routledge and Kegan
Paul.

Tibble, J.W. (1966b). Introduction. In J.W. Tibble (Ed.), *The study of education*
(pp. vii–x). London: Routledge and Kegan Paul.

Tibble, J.W. (1966c). The development of the study of education. In J.W. Tibble (Ed.),
The study of education (pp. 1–28). London: Routledge and Kegan Paul.

Tibble, J.W. (Ed.) (1971a). *An introduction to the study of education*. London:
Routledge and Kegan Paul.

Tibble, J.W. (1971b). The development of the study of education. In J.W. Tibble (Ed.),
An introduction to the study of education (pp. 5–17). London: Routledge and
Kegan Paul.

Townsend, T. (Ed.) (2007). *International handbook of school effectiveness and school
improvement*. Dordrecht/Boston: Springer.

Trapp, E.C. (1778). *Von der Beförderung der wirksamen Erkenntniß*. Itzehoe: Müller.

Trapp, E.C. (1779). *Von der Nothwendigkeit, Erziehen und Unterrichten als eine eigene
Kunst zu studieren*. Antrittsvorlesung Universität Halle. Halle: J.C. Hendel.

Vries, G.H. de (1990). *De ontwikkeling van Wetenschap. [The development of science.]*
Groningen: Wolters-Noordhoff.

Weiss, C.H., Murphy-Graham, E., Petrosino, A. & Gandhi, A.G. (2008). The fairy
godmother – and her warts: Making the dream of evidence-based policy come
true. *American Journal of Evaluation 29*(1), 29–47.

Wellcome Trust. (2003). *Economic analysis of scientific research publishing*.
Cambridge: The Wellcome Trust. Available online at: http://www.wellcome.ac.uk/
doc_WTD003181.html.

Westbury, I. (2007). Theory and theorizing in curriculum studies. In E. Forsberg
(Ed.), *Curriculum theory revisited* (pp.1–19). Uppsala: Uppsala University.

Westbury, I. & Wilkof, N. (Eds.) (1978). *Science, curriculum, and liberal education: Selected essays*. Chicago: The University of Chicago Press.

Willinsky, J. (2006). *The access principle: The case for open research and scholarship*. Cambridge, MA: MIT Press.

Wiseman, A.W. (2010). The uses of evidence for educational policymaking: Global contexts and international trends. *Review of Research in Education 34*(1), 1–24.

Woolgar, S. (1988). *Science, the very idea*. Chichester: Tavistock Books.

Wulf, Chr. (1978). *Theorien und Konzepte der Erziehungswissenschaft*. München: Juventa.

Index